A Whale Watcher's Cookbook

Views from the Galley

A Whale Watcher's Cookbook

Views from the Galley

by Sharon Nogg

Media Publishing
A Division of Westport Publishers, Inc.

Illustrations: Kelley Balcomb-Bartok

Cover Photo: Sharon Nogg

Cover Design: Noelle M. Kaplan, finedesign

ISBN 0-939644-66-5

Printed in the United States of America.

Media Publishing
A Division of Westport Publishers, Inc.
2440 'O' Street, Suite 202
Lincoln, Nebraska

To My Parents

Three years ago, during the first Earth Watch session in Washington, one of the volunteers said, "Sharon, all of your recipes are so good you should write a cookbook."

I casually mentioned her remark to Mom and that was the beginning.

If not for her many hours of work and perseverence, this cookbook would never have happened.

And a special thanks to Dad for eating all those TV dinners while Mom was busy at the computer.

And to Ken Balcomb for helping me get started in my career with whales.

Table of Contents

BREAKFAST

SOUPS

SALADS

FISH AND SEAFOOD

CHICKEN

MEAT

VEGETABLES AND SIDE DISHES

DESSERTS

HINTS FOR SEASONING WITHOUT SALT

ABOUT THE AUTHOR

FOREWORD

Okay, we have decided we simply must do something to help Mother Earth and the creatures that live upon it. Maybe we are going to save whales, maybe we are going to save trees, or maybe we want to learn about natural processes that are essential to life as we know it on this planet.

Whatever our reason, we have made a commitment to **DO** something and we cannot do it alone. So we organize; we gather with like-minded folks and set out to do what we think is important. We work, study, and learn we really can accomplish great things with our combined efforts toward a common goal.

But sooner or later, we have to pause to eat. And that is how this book came about. It started with an ORCA Survey (a study of killer whales in the Pacific Northwest), teams of volunteers from EARTHWATCH (an organization that sends professional and lay people to help with ecology and scientific projects around the world) and Sharon Nogg.

The job of feeding up to 20 people three times a day, along with research chores, overwhelmed her. She masterminded and coordinated the shopping and cooking game plan but we decided early on that no one person could be solely responsible for preparing all the meals—they'd get burned out.

So, armed with a variety of recipes, and by rotating the cooking chores, things worked out well.

The result of all this input is a cookbook that has something for every taste. Many of the recipes have since been used at sea and in remote locations.

My thanks to Sharon Nogg for keeping up with this effort and getting this book to print.

Kenneth C. Balcomb
Vice President
Center for Whale Research
Friday Harbor, WA

Co-Author of
WHALES OF THE WORLD

PREFACE

Three and a half years ago I decided I was tired of the rat race in Los Angeles. While I enjoyed my work with the American Humane Association, I needed a change. Boy did I get one!

I went from a "normal" 40 hour a week job and a permanent home, to picking up and moving every four or five months, to follow the whales and the job.

I was very fortunate to hear about Ken Balcomb and the work he does in Washington state with Orcas or Killer Whales. While I had been involved working with animals for over five years, I had no experience with whales. There is no question, Ken hired me for my knowledge in the kitchen rather than for my knowledge and experience with whales.

From the time I was a little girl I remember spending hours in the kitchen with my Mom, one of my grandmothers or my great-grandmother.

However, planning menus to feed fifteen people at a time, on a budget, and with recipes that anyone, from a professional chef to a "noncook" could easily make, was not something that I had ever contemplated doing.

To complicate things a little more, we were on a small island where groceries are very expensive. So the idea was to plan ahead so that most of the shopping could be done once every two weeks or so in Seattle.

I looked around for cookbooks that featured gourmet meals that were easy to prepare and inexpensive to make. Having no luck from family and friends. That first summer I shared my recipes with a lot of people. At one point someone suggested, since people always wanted my recipes, I should write a cookbook. At that point I wasn't sure that I had enough recipes for one book.

That thought was to change with my job the following summer.

I was working on Ken Balcomb's project in Washington again, when I was offered a job working as a cook for 13 people on Tonn Storro Patterson's boat DELPHINUS in southeast Alaska.

When Ron offered me the job I was a bit reluctant. After all, I wanted to spend time on a boat photographing whales, not cooking.

Once again I have Ken Balcomb to thank. He encouraged me to take the job. As he said, the important things was to get up to southeast Alaska to gain some knowledge of the area, as well as experience the incredible beauty along the inside passage.

When I accepted the job I made up my mind, I was going to be very well organized, and use recipes that could be prepared ahead of time or quickly at the last minute. Most important to me, along with preparing delicious meals, was to be able to go outside and photograph whales when they were near our boat, or be free to go ashore to hike on the islands along with our passengers rather than spend all day in the galley. Of course, I had to keep in mind that the passengers on DELPHINUS were spending enough money on their vacation that they should have, if not a 10-course gourmet feast, at least more than a piece of broiled chicken and a baked potato.

The problems that I had were not coming up with recipes. Again, some revising of my favorite recipes and help from friends and family made that part of the job easy. But first, I had to get accustomed to a galley that barely held two people, (two fairly thin people at that). Of course that meant VERY little work space. And add to that a small oven (room for a 10–12 pound turkey only; any bigger and it would not fit). And a 4 burner stove that had the interesting feature of having only 2 working burners when the oven was on.

Another dilemma that fortunately Ron had worked out long ago, was storage of perishable foods. There was no space in the galley for even a normal size refrigerator/freezer. By the time I had put milk, cream, butter, and cream cheese in the refrigerator, it was full. Keep in mind we were going on a week to ten day cruise and had no opportunity to go shopping during the trips.

The solution to the problem? We used coolers (like the ones you take to the beach or camping, only much larger). Of course we could not fill them with regular ice, it melts too quickly, and we would not be able to replace it during the trip. The solution is easy, if you happen to be cruising in waters near a glacier. Simply get in the Zodiac (a small rubber dingy) armed with a large fishing net and go and round up some small icebergs. You see, because glacial ice is incredibly dense, it melts very slowly. Ice gathered at the beginning of a cruise would last for the entire voyage.

After three months of cooking on DELPHINUS I began to think that perhaps I would write a cookbook.

I no longer cook for a living. Thanks to the wonderful experience I gained in Washington and southeast Alaska I am now able to work as a naturalist.

Spending days talking to people about whales and the natural history of Hawaii and Alaska is a wonderful way to earn a living. And while I occasionally miss the cooking, I never miss having to do the dishes.

Sharon Nogg
Honolulu, Hawaii

ACKNOWLEDGEMENTS

I wish to thank the following people and organizations for sharing their recipes with me.

Alaska Fish & Wildlife Department
National Fisheries Institute
Bobbi Saper
Barbara Frankel
Suzanne Sawin
Sheila Rosen
Ted Rogers
Liz Kreekos
Mrs. Bernard Schimmel
Ruth Nogg
Eileen Nogg
Sitka's Russian Folk Dancers
Jaki Eyre
Julie Johnson
Esther Rice
Don Remacle
Norman Siegel
Jim Welch
Mabel Rips
Ann Landers
and Bubi *who was one of the best cooks in the world but never had a real recipe.*

APPETIZERS

The first line of this section seems as good a place as any to tell you that unless the recipe cautions you not to use substitutes, cheeses, butter and eggs can be replaced with artificial ingredients without sacrificing too much, if any flavor.

Some of the dishes in this chapter can also be used for light lunches or a main course by adding vegetables and salad.

Bacon-Wrapped Crackers

Box of Waverly-type crackers
1 pound bacon
Honey

Separate crackers. Cut bacon strips in half. Wrap a piece of bacon around each cracker. Brush each wrapped cracker with honey.

Bake at 350° turning once, until bacon is well cooked but not too crisp. Serve warm.

Serves 8–10.

Bacon Twists

6 slices stale white bread; if not stale freeze for a few minutes until firm. Trim crusts.
3 ounces cream cheese, softened
1 tablespoon mayonnaise
1/4–1/2 teaspoon onion powder
1/4–1/2 teaspoon seasoning salt
9 slices of bacon, cut in half.

Combine mayonnaise, cheese, onion and seasoning salt. Blend thoroughly. Spread on bread. Place in refrigerator to harden. Cut each slice into three strips. Wrap bacon in spirals around each strip of bread. Fasten with a toothpick.

Place under broiler for approximately 10 minutes, turning once, or until bacon is crisp.

Serves 4–6.

Bacon and Onion Cheesecake

1 cup stale wholegrain bread crumbs
6 slices of bacon (about 1 cup) chopped
1 onion, chopped
1 clove minced garlic
12 ounces cream cheese
1 tablespoon flour
4 eggs, lightly beaten
6 or 8 ounces sour cream

Press bread crumbs over base of greased springform pan. Cook bacon and onion in pan for about 5 minutes or until brown. Add garlic, drain excess grease and cool. Beat cream cheese and flour in medium bowl with electric mixer until smooth, then beat in eggs and sour cream. Stir bacon mixture into cream cheese mixture, pour into pan. Place on cookie sheet and bake at 325° for 40 minutes or until set. Cool 10 minutes before removing from pan.

Serves 6.

The word "whale" means great fish, but whales aren't fish, they're mammals.

Crab Meat Muffins

4 English muffins, split
2 tablespoons butter or margarine
1/2 pound mushrooms, sliced or chopped
1 pound crab meat or imitation crab meat
1 cup fresh bread crumbs
2 tablespoons chopped dill, optional, or to taste
Salt and white pepper to taste
2 1/2 cups white cream sauce

Split English muffins and toast lightly. Butter muffins generously, butter should be absorbed into muffins. Chop mushrooms and sauté in butter. Add mushrooms and crab meat to cream sauce. Pile crab meat mixture onto muffins, add bread crumbs and dot with butter. Use a sharp knife to cut into four sections for finger food (as a first course, serve whole).

Bake in preheated oven 350° for about 15 minutes.

You may prepare these ahead of time and bake when ready to serve.

Garnish

Bake the muffins for about 10–12 minutes.

Add thinly sliced Jack cheese and place under broiler for a few minutes, until cheese melts.

You can also dust with paprika or sprinkle snips of parsley or dill on top.

These are very rich. Half a muffin is enough for most people.

Serves 2–4.

Baked Crab Meat Puff

You may substitute small shrimp or tuna for crab meat.

12 slices white bread, crusts removed
6 slices Jack or Colby cheese
2 cups imitation or real crab meat
3 eggs
2 cups milk
Salt and pepper to taste

Arrange 6 slices of bread across bottom of a buttered 9" x 13" pan. Place a slice of cheese over each piece of bread. Cover the cheese with crab meat, spread evenly over each slice of bread. Top with remaining slices of bread.

Beat eggs with milk, salt and pepper. Pour over bread. Chill for at least two hours. Can be made ahead and refrigerated. Seal with plastic wrap until ready to bake.

Bake in a 350° oven for 30 minutes or until puffed up like a soufflé. Serve immediately.

Serves 6.

Egg Salad # 1

All of these spreads can be served with crackers or cocktail breads as appetizers or as sandwiches.

1 dozen hard boiled eggs, chopped
4 stalks of celery, chopped
1 small red onion, chopped
1 sweet red pepper, seeded and chopped
1 tablespoon sweet paprika
1/2 cup sour cream
1/2 cup mayonnaise
Salt and pepper to taste

Mix sour cream, mayonnaise, paprika, salt and pepper. Blend into all other ingredients.

Egg Salad # 2

1 dozen hard boiled eggs, chopped
4 stalks of celery, chopped
3/4 to 1 cup mayonnaise
2 teaspoons curry powder or to taste
3 scallions, chopped

Mix all ingredients together.

Egg Salad # 3

1 dozen hard boiled eggs, chopped
4 stalks of celery
3 green onions, chopped
12 ounces of bacon, cooked crisp, drained and crumbled
2 to 3 tablespoons prepared white horseradish, drained
3/4 to 1 cup mayonnaise
Salt and pepper to taste

Mix horseradish and mayonnaise together. Blend with all other ingredients.

Dilled Meatballs

2 pounds hamburger
1/2 cup evaporated milk
1/2 cup uncooked instant or fast cook oatmeal
1/2 cup sour cream (double amount if you want more gravy)
1 tablespoon dill
1/2 teaspoon lemon juice

Mix first three ingredients, then roll into balls about the size of a walnut. Lightly brown in a fry pan. Drain excess fat and push to side of pan. Stir in sour cream, dill and lemon juice. Blend with meatballs. Simmer to heat thoroughly.

You may use rye or caraway seeds in place of dill.

If you wish to serve it as a main dish, place on a bed of rice or noodles.

Serves 4.

HINT: Meatballs for this and the following dish can be frozen. Defrost and then add the sauce.

Curried Meatballs

Use above recipe for meatballs.

To a standard white cream sauce stir in 1/2 teaspoon to 1 tablespoon of curry powder, depending on personal taste.

Serve over rice.

This is a colorful dish and offers guests an unexpected taste treat.
Serves 4.

NOTE: Undiluted soup, such as Cream of Celery, can be substituted for part of the sour cream in these meatball sauces.

Whales' Tails*

4 ounces Parmesan or Romano cheese, grated
4 tablespoons low calorie margarine
2 tablespoons skim milk
8 large whole wheat pita breads (pocket bread)

While easier to prepare in a food processor, as I discovered when cooking on the *DELPHINUS*, may be done by hand.

Mix cheese, margarine and milk preparation to spreading consistency. Cut pita bread into quarters. Separate bottom and top of each quarter, making 64 triangles. Spread each triangle with cheese mixture and bake on ungreased baking sheets at 350° until lightly browned.

You can make cheese mix ahead and keep in refrigerator for several days. Prepared triangles can be frozen, then baked after thawing.

One of the little children on board thought two of these side by side looked like the whales' tails we had been studying—the name stuck. And good news for dieters—only 25 calories each!

Makes 64.

Herbed Bread Sticks

1 loaf French bread, unsliced
1 cup butter or margarine, softened
1/2 teaspoon dried tarragon
1 teaspoon dried basil
1/2 teaspoon oregano
1/2 teaspoon garlic powder
1 teaspoon onion powder

Cut the bread into 6" long thin sticks. Combine the remaining ingredients. Spread on all sides of the bread. Place on cookie sheet, covered with foil. Bake at 350° for about 6–7 minutes or until golden brown, turning once.

Experiment with different herbs to create your own combinations. If you like cheese, sprinkle with a dusting of grated cheese.

Makes 2 dozen.

Salmon Mousse

I use this as an appetizer at cocktail parties but it also is good as a luncheon main dish.

2 cups salmon, crushed to fine texture
1 tablespoon chopped capers
1 tablespoon onion, or chives (optional)
1/2 cup mayonnaise
1 tablespoon lemon juice
1/2 teaspoon Tabasco sauce
1 teaspoon paprika
1/4 teaspoon salt
1 envelope unflavored gelatin
1 cup boiling hot water
1/2 cup cold water

Dissolve gelatin in hot water, stir until dissolved, then add cold water (if a firmer mold is desired, reduce hot water to 1/2 cup and cold water to 1/4 cup). Note: gelatin can be temperamental, especially in damp climates. I did have trouble making some gelatin dishes when I cooked on the converted trawler. When I have trouble with the gelatin setting, I simply serve it as a dip with vegetables or chips.

Mash the salmon, after removing any bones. Mix with the mayonnaise until it forms a thick paste. Add the remaining ingredients and blend thoroughly. Chill for at least 4 hours in oiled mold.

If you choose to make a creamier mix, it will spread more like a pâté.

Presentation for Salmon Mousse

Use a fish-shaped mold; after unmolding, place a slice of black or green olive on mousse to form an "eye."

Apply thinly sliced, well-drained cucumber slices in overlapping "petals" to form scales and cover entire mold.

If you do not have a fish mold, use a canister shape, then slice and serve on lettuce or spinach leaves as a first course.

Place dollop of sour cream mixture in center and if you want it to really be festive, sprinkle black caviar over sour cream.

For Savory Sour Cream Sauce, mix:

1 cup dairy sour cream
1 teaspoon chopped dill weed
1 1/2 teaspoons lemon juice

Serve in a side dish.

This mousse may be served on crackers or thinly sliced cocktail bread especially rye flavored.

Serves 8–10 appetizer servings.

I love to travel and have been blessed with some wonderful opportunities to see the world and sample simple but exotic foods. As a student aboard the World Campus Afloat's S.S. UNIVERSE, I not only had a chance to eat in a variety of countries on our around-the-world odyssey, but occasionally the cook would try to create a culinary adaption that we might take home with us.

Since this appetizer can be made a day ahead, it's a good one for a harried party-giver.

East Indian Cream Cheese Spread

8 ounces cream cheese, softened
3 tablespoons curry powder
3 green onions, chopped fine
1/3 cup sour cream
8 ounces chutney
2/3 cup peanuts, chopped

Mix together cream cheese and sour cream. Add curry powder and green onions. Pour into container and chill for at least 4 hours.

Invert onto a serving plate. Cover with chutney and sprinkle peanuts over top. Serve with assorted crackers.

Serves 8.

Super Easy and Quick Cream Cheese Appetizer

8 ounces cream cheese
6 ounces Jalapeno pepper jelly OR
6 ounces chutney OR
6 ounces salsa

Simply pour any one of the above ingredients over the cream cheese block and serve with crackers.

If you need something in a hurry or you have no time for anything fancy, this is it. The Jalapeno Pepper jelly version is the first thing I run out of at parties.

Serves 4–6.

Baked Cream Cheese with Sesame Seeds

8 ounces cream cheese, softened
Sesame seeds

Roll cream cheese into a ball, then roll in sesame seeds. (As a block, "frost" the sides and top with seeds.)

Bake on an ungreased cookie sheet at 325° for 1 hour so that the seeds are lightly browned.

The cheese will puff as it bakes and may be very creamy. Serve with crackers.

So simple yet I have never served it at a party that someone does not ask for the recipe.

Serves 4–6.

Cheese Puff Cubes

1 loaf white bread, sliced
3 ounces cream cheese
1/4 pound sharp cheddar cheese
1/2 cup butter or margarine
2 egg whites, beaten stiff

Remove crust from bread and cut into 1 inch cubes. Melt cheeses and butter in top of a double boiler to keep from scorching.

Fold stiffly beaten egg whites into blended cheese mixture. Dip bread cubes into the mixture.

Place on a cookie sheet and refrigerate overnight. Preheat oven to 400° and bake for 10 minutes, until puffy.

Makes about 10 dozen.

Red and White Cream Cheese Loaf

8 ounces block of cream cheese
3/4 cup chili sauce
1/2 teaspoon Tabasco
1 cup shrimp, flaked crab or lobster
   (imitation works well also)

Mix well then "frost" 8 ounce block of cream cheese. Serve with cocktail rye bread or rye crackers.

Serves 6.

Hawaiian Chicken Cubes

1 pound boned and skinned chicken breasts
1/4 cup lemon juice
3 tablespoons Worcestershire sauce
1/2 cup flour
1 egg, beaten
1/2 cup unseasoned bread crumbs
1/2 cup crushed macadamia nuts

Cut chicken into 1 inch cubes. Place in bowl containing lemon juice and Worcestershire sauce. Marinate for one hour.

Take 3 bowls and put flour in one, egg in another and mix nuts and bread crumbs in the third bowl.

Remove chicken from marinade. Dip chicken first in flour, then in egg; coat with nut-crumb mixture.

Place in single layer on a greased shallow baking pan. Bake, uncovered, in a preheated 350° oven until chicken is cooked and lightly browned, about 25 minutes.

Skewer on toothpicks with pineapple cubes.

You can use a variety of dipping sauces but this one is a little different.

Chutney Sauce

3/4 cup mayonnaise
1/4 cup mustard
3 tablespoons chutney, chopped

Combine and refrigerate to blend flavors.

Serves 4.

Wine Camembert

This appetizer works best if left to marinate overnight, or at least five to six hours.

1 small Camembert
3/4 cup dry white wine
4 ounces butter (do not substitute margarine)
3–4 drops Tabasco sauce
3 ounces sliced almonds, toasted lightly

Place cheese in a small bowl. Cover with wine. Marinate.

Drain wine and chop cheese, including rind, into 5 or 6 pieces. Add softened butter and Tabasco sauce. Beat on medium speed until well blended and very smooth.

Chill for about 10 minutes, then pat cheese back into original shape.

Roll top and sides of cheese ball in almonds. Chill until firm.

Remove from refrigerator about 30 minutes before serving.

Serves 6.

Whales are warm blooded and breathe air.

BREADS

Cheesy Bread Sticks

These are great served with soup.

   1 1/2 cups Parmesan or Romano cheese, grated
   1/2 cup sesame seeds
   1 cup butter or margarine, melted
   1 pound white bread loaf

Combine cheese and sesame seeds. Trim crusts from bread and cut each slice into thirds. Dip each slice in butter and roll in cheese and sesame seed mixture. Place on a cookie sheet and broil on each side until lightly browned. May be frozen. Place on cookie sheet and bake at 325° until heated thoroughly.

Serves 12–15.

Herbed Cracker Bread (Lavosh)

This is a nice alternative to plain crackers.

   1 package of Lavosh (Cracker Bread)
   Margarine or butter, melted
   Basil, tarragon or dill

Brush melted margarine on top of each piece of lavosh. Sprinkle with any combination of herbs that you like. Place under broiler just long enough to brown lightly. Cool and break into pieces.

Depending on how many Lavosh are in package and if large crackers or bite size, allow 3–4 small crackers per person or 1 large cracker for 2–3 people.

Curry Mayonnaise Toast

This bread is great with soups or as an appetizer.

6 slices white bread
2 ounces butter or margarine
2 tablespoons mayonnaise
2 teaspoons curry powder
3 tablespoons grated Parmesan cheese
Paprika

Remove crust from bread, toast one side. Combine remaining ingredients except paprika. Spread evenly over untoasted side of bread slices. Sprinkle with paprika.

Cut each slice evenly into thirds. Place on baking sheet.

Bake at 350° for 15–20 minutes or until golden brown.

Serves 6.

All whales—including porpoises and dolphins—are known collectively as cetaceans.

Alaskan Ice Cream Muffins

Strange as it may sound, the ice cream in this recipe simply replaces regular liquid. The muffins are on the bland side, so you can butter them. You can also enhance the flavor by experimenting with flavorings of your choice.

1 1/2 cups flour—plain or self-raising
1 tablespoon baking powder (omit if using self-rising flour)
1 teaspoon salt (omit if using self-rising flour)
1 egg
2 tablespoons cooking oil
2 cups vanilla ice cream, softened (I have also used peach ice cream)

Measure dry ingredients into a mixing bowl. Put moist ingredients in another bowl and blend. Form a depression in the dry ingredient bowl and add the wet mixture. Mix only until dry particles are moistened.

Bake in well greased muffin cups, 3/4 full at 425° for 20 minutes or until golden brown.

NOTE: This is a fairly hot oven so you need to keep an eye on them to be sure they don't overbake.

Oat Bran and Raisin Muffins

2 cups oat bran, uncooked
2 teaspoons baking powder
1 teaspoons cinnamon
1/3 teaspoons nutmeg
1 cup milk
1/3 cup honey
1/4 cup vegetable oil
2 egg whites
1 cup seedless raisins

Mix first four ingredients in a large bowl. In a small bowl, beat milk, oil, honey, and egg whites until well blended; add oat bran mixture and stir just until oat bran is moistened. Do not over mix. Fold in raisins. Spoon batter into 12 paper-lined muffin tin cups. Bake in a 425° oven for 20 minutes, or until a toothpick inserted into the center of the muffin comes out clean. Remove muffins from the tin immediately and cool on a wire rack.

Sour Cream Raisin Muffins

1 cup flour
1/2 teaspoon baking powder
1/2 teaspoon baking soda
1/4 teaspoon salt
1/2 teaspoon cinnamon
1/4 teaspoon nutmeg
1 large egg
3/4 cup sour cream
1/2 cup raisins
1/2 cup brown sugar
1 cup chopped walnuts, optional

Mix together flour, soda, baking powder, salt, and spices. In a medium bowl beat egg; add sugar and sour cream and beat until well blended. Add the flour mixture, raisins and nuts. Stir only until batter is moistened yet lumpy. Fill 12 muffin cups 3/4 full. Bake at 350° for about 25 minutes.

Blueberry Muffins

Long before canning and freezing processes were invented, the Micmac Indians sun-dried blueberries to preserve them. They make a great snack for dieters as they are low in calories and sodium and have no cholesterol.

A hot blueberry muffin is a great way to start the day. Even though this recipe is easy, I often measure out all the dry ingredients the night before. While the oven preheats, I mix the remaining items and bake while fixing the rest of the breakfast meal.

2 cups flour
1/2 cup sugar
1 tablespoon baking powder
1 cup milk
1/2 cup melted butter or margarine
1 egg
1/2 teaspoon salt
1 cup fresh or frozen blueberries

Stir dry ingredients together and gently add blueberries.

Combine egg, milk and margarine. Add to blueberry mix, stirring just enough to moisten. **Do not beat.** Spoon batter into 12 muffin cups.

Bake at 375° for 20 minutes.

Zucchini Nut Bread

4 cups grated zucchini, peeled and drained
3 1/2 cups sugar
6 eggs
2 cups oil
2 teaspoons vanilla
6 cups flour
1 teaspoon salt
2 teaspoons soda
2 teaspoons nutmeg
1 tablespoon cinnamon
3/4 cup finely chopped nuts

Blend together all wet ingredients. Sift together and add the dry ingredients. Fold in nuts. Bake for 55 to 60 minutes at 350° degrees.

Makes three loaves.

Pumpkin Bread

1 cup brown sugar
3/4 cup granulated sugar
4 eggs
1 cup oil
2 cups pumpkin purèe
3 cups unbleached flour
1/2 cup whole wheat flour
2 teaspoons soda
1/2 teaspoon salt
1 teaspoon cinnamon
1/2 teaspoon nutmeg
1/2 teaspoon allspice
1/2 teaspoon ground cloves

Combine both sugars, eggs, oil and pumpkin. Mix well. Add both flours, soda, salt and spices. Mix thoroughly. Bake at 350° for 1 hour.

Makes two loaves.

Banana Nut Bread

1/2 cup butter or margarine
1 cup sugar
2 eggs, beaten
3 very ripe bananas, mashed
2 cups flour, sifted
1 teaspoon baking soda
1/4 cup walnuts, chopped

Mix the ingredients together in the order given. Stir until well blended. Bake in a loaf pan at 350° for 50–60 minutes.

Apple Bread

1 1/2 cups vegetable oil
1 3/4 cups sugar
3 eggs
3 cups flour
1 1/2 teaspoons baking soda
1/2 teaspoon cinnamon
1/2 teaspoon nutmeg
1/2 teaspoon ground cloves
1 teaspoon vanilla
3 cups apples, peeled and diced

Combine oil and sugar and beat until light and fluffy. Add eggs and beat well. Combine the dry ingredients and add to the egg mixture. Stir in the vanilla and apples.

Pour into a greased bundt pan and bake at 350° for 1 hour and 15 minutes. Cool 10 minutes and remove from pan.

Carrot Bread

4 eggs
2 cups sugar
1 1/4 cup salad oil
3 cups unsifted flour
1 1/2 teaspoon soda
1/8 teaspoon salt
1 teaspoon cinnamon
2 teaspoons baking powder
2 cups shredded carrots, (as thin as possible)

Beat eggs, add sugar gradually, beating until thickened. Gradually add oil and beat until thoroughly mixed. Stir in dry ingredients. Add carrots and stir until well blended.

Use 5" x 9" well-greased loaf pans.

Bake for one hour at 350°.

Makes two loaves.

Cheese and Onion Bread

1 cup grated cheese—Jack, Cheddar or Jalapeno Jack
1 1/2 cups biscuit mix
1 tablespoon dry minced onion
2 tablespoons margarine, melted
1 egg
1/2 cup milk
1 teaspoon caraway or rye seeds

Mix margarine and onion.

Blend biscuit mix thoroughly with the grated cheese. Mix together and add remaining ingredients.

Use a flat 8" square pan rather than a bread loaf pan for this recipe.

Bake for 20 minutes in a 375° oven.

Sperm whales are the largest of the toothed whales—
they can be up to 60 feet long.

Cornbread

1 1/2 cups cornmeal
1 1/2 cups flour
3/4 cup sugar
1 1/2 tablespoons baking powder
3/4 teaspoon salt, optional
3/4 cup vegetable oil
2 eggs
1 cup milk and 1 cup buttermilk OR 2 cups milk

Mix dry ingredients in a large bowl.

Beat eggs and oil together, add to milk. Pour into dry ingredients and stir until completely blended.

Bake in a greased 9" x 13" pan for about 25 minutes at 350°.

This is excellent served with chili or beef stew.

Beer Bread

3 cups self-rising flour
3 tablespoons sesame seeds
3 tablespoons sugar
1 12 ounce can of beer, room temperature

Mix flour, sesame seeds, and sugar together until blended. Add the beer and mix well. Pour into a greased 8" pie pan or an 8" square pan. Bake for 60 minutes at 350°.

NOTE: This is a very crisp bread that is great with soups. If you want a softer bread, add 3 tablespoons of vegetable oil.

Popovers

1 cup flour
1/2 teaspoon salt
1 tablespoon shortening
2 large eggs
1 cup milk

Eggs and milk should be at room temperature.

Mix all ingredients together in a bowl and beat with a wire whip or wooden spoon. Do not use an electric mixer.

Spoon batter into 8 large, greased custard cups or greased muffin tin. Bake 50 minutes at 375°. Remove from oven. Quickly slit side of each popover to allow the steam to escape. Return to oven for 10 minutes.

Remove from cups or muffin tin immediately.

Hole in the Middle Bread

I like to bake bread, but rarely bother to take the time to do it from scratch. There are good frozen loaves that rise as they are defrosting. Then all you have to do is pop them in the oven.

Most of the time, I make slits in the dough as it starts to rise. These narrow openings can be filled with a variety of grated cheeses, melted herb butter or any concoction that suits you. A great favorite with most people is dough that's brushed with melted butter or margarine and sprinkled with Parmesan cheese before baking.

So where does the hole come in? In the middle like it says!

Either bake or buy small round rye bread. You may use other flavors but they are softer in texture and don't always work as well.

Scoop out the center so you have a hole about the size of a coffee cup. You must leave a "wall" at least an inch thick around the opening. Let loaf dry out or put in microwave—we all know how fast that can dry out bread!

Heat any of the following and fill hole, serve immediately.

Serve the bread chunks along with the soup or stew. And if you are agile enough, you can break off pieces from the shell as you go along.

French Onion Soup—be sure your broth is not watery. Bring shredded cheese to room temperate before filling shell. Pour in soup, top with onions and sprinkle with cheese. Pop under pre-heated broiler for a minute to melt cheese.

Beef or Chicken Stew

Cream of Chicken Soup with Vegetables

Any thick soup

This is a fun dish for a cold day in front of the fire. It's very filling and with a salad you have a complete meal.

BREAKFAST

Swiss Eggs

4 eggs
4 thin slices cheddar cheese
1 tablespoon butter
2 tablespoons grated cheddar or Swiss cheese
3 tablespoons half and half or cream
Salt and pepper to taste
Paprika

Melt butter in bottom of a small baking dish or casserole. Cover with cheese slices. Gently drop an egg onto each slice of cheese. Pour the cream over eggs. Season with salt and pepper.

Top with grated cheese and sprinkle with paprika.

Bake at 350° until eggs are set and cheese is light brown.

Breakfast on the Run

This mixture has an unexpected ingredient for a breakfast dish. And while you can certainly sit and enjoy it at the breakfast table, if you're an eat-and-run person, you can take it with you when you use bread or muffins as your "sandwich."

4 hard-boiled eggs, chopped
1/4 cup shredded cheddar cheese
2 1/2 tablespoons bottled bacon and tomato flavored dressing
2–4 toasted, bread slices, waffles or English muffin halves
Thin tomato slices (optional)

Mix eggs, cheese and dressing together. Cover and chill to blend flavors. Spread half the mix on the waffle base. In oven or toaster oven, broil six inches from heat until warm (about three minutes).

Top with additional waffles and garnish with tomato slices and parsley if you wish. For a breakfast on the run, spread mixture on muffin or bread. Heat or not, as you prefer.

Walking Breakfast–Hollywood Style

For several years I worked as an animal protection officer on television and motion picture sets. Whether shooting in Hollywood or on location, the caterers always had what was known as "walking breakfasts." With crews starting as early as four or five in the morning, food had to be readily available and sometimes you really had to eat on the run.

While menus could vary from caterer to caterer, this dish seemed to be used by most of them.

To warmed, soft tortillas add:

Scrambled eggs
Grated cheese
Cooked sausage or bacon

Roll up and eat as you would a sandwich. Add refried beans, salsa and onions for more of a Mexican-type meal.

Egg 'n Cheese Strata

6 slices bread (better if day old)
3 tablespoons softened butter or margarine
1 cup shredded cheddar cheese
6 eggs, slightly beaten
1 1/2 cups milk
1 teaspoon dry mustard
1/2 teaspoon salt

Butter bread and cut into small cubes. Alternate layers of bread cubes and cheese in buttered 2 quart casserole.

Blend together eggs, milk and seasonings. Pour over bread and cheese.

Cover and refrigerate for several hours. May be refrigerated overnight. (I feel it rises into a lighter dish if you let it sit out for 15–20 minutes before baking.)

Bake in preheated 350° oven for 20 minutes or until golden brown.

This basic recipe serves 4–6.

Variations—According to your taste, you can add a cup or two of shredded crab meat or shrimp, leftover chicken, turkey, ham or bacon. This is a great dish to experiment with as the basic mixture blends well with a variety of other foods.

Frittatas Galore

A frittata is the Italian version of an omelet—the chief difference is that it is heavier and deliberately cooked to a firm texture.

Frittatas are great for breakfast, brunch or a light supper.

For best results, always cook egg dishes over low heat so they don't overcook. The ideal frittata will still be a smidge moist inside and have a firm, but not tough, outside.

Basic Frittata

> **6 eggs**
> **2 tablespoons grated Parmesan cheese**
> **Salt and pepper to taste**

Stir ingredients until blended (eggs should not be foamy).

Add whatever filling you are using and stir to mix.

In 9" or 10" skillet heat oil or margarine to sizzling, then tip the pan to coat the sides.

Pour in egg mixture and immediately stir gently three or four times—**do not stir like scrambled eggs**. With a fork or spatula, lift edges of omelet and allow uncooked part to run underneath.

Cook until edge is golden brown and center is firm. If edge is browning too fast and center is still moist, place under the broiler for a minute or two.

Some frittata recipes call for turning the omelet over to brown on the other side. There's nothing wrong with that approach except many times the ingredients rise to the top and form an attractive pattern. It's not quite as pretty if you then turn it over but either way, it tastes wonderful.

Normally frittatas are cut into pie-shaped wedges, or cut into squares and used for snacks.

Mushroom and Spinach mix
6–8 ounces sliced mushrooms, fresh or canned
1/4 cup minced onion
1 package (10 ounce) frozen, chopped spinach, thawed
1/4 teaspoon salt

Sauté mushrooms and onions in margarine or olive oil for about 5 minutes. Stir in spinach, then blend with basic egg mixture.

Heat as directed above. Turn onto warmed platter, cut into wedges.

Serves 4-6.

Frittata a la Formaggio mix
Add to egg mix:
1 tablespoon water
1/8 teaspoon oregano
3/4 cup diced Bel Paese cheese
1 tablespoon minced parsley
Salt and pepper to taste

Cook as above.

Other Vegetables
Zucchini slices
Drained, sliced firm tomatoes
Any sliced, cooked meats
Cheeses:
    1/2 cup ricotta cheese
    1/2 cup cottage cheese, drained
    1/2 cup any firm cheese, diced or grated

While frittatas do not need a sauce, there's a restaurant in Beverly Hills that serves their zucchini and cheese frittata with a hot salsa. If hot sauces are to your taste, you could use a taco style or picante salsa.

Elegant, Easy Eggs Baked in a Crust

6 frozen patty shells
6 eggs
1/2 cup dairy sour cream, scant
2 ounce can drained mushrooms
1/4 teaspoon dill weed
Dash salt

Bake patty shells according to directions on the package BUT REMOVE from oven after 20 minutes.

Reduce temperature to 375°.

Carefully remove tops and soft pastry underneath, set aside.

Gently break an egg and slip one into each shell. Bake until white is almost set, about 14–15 minutes.

While eggs are cooking, blend sour cream, mushroom and seasonings together.

When you remove egg filled shells from oven, spoon about two tablespoons of cream mix over each egg. Continue baking for about three minutes, until hot. Pastry tops can serve as a lid. Can be garnished with spring of fresh dill.

Serves 6.

Hawaiian Baked Eggs

I suspect that hidden somewhere in the middle of a cane field lies a little man or woman whose sole purpose in life is to dream up new recipes using pineapple. The fact that some of these recipes are right off the wall, adds to the charm.

1 pound can crushed, drained pineapple
3 cups cooked rice
1/2 cup sour cream
1/2 cup grated Swiss cheese
1/2 tablespoon chopped onion (optional)
1 tablespoon finely chopped parsley
6 eggs
Dash Tabasco sauce
Salt and pepper to personal taste

Combine all ingredients, **except** eggs. Spoon into 6 greased, individual baking cups.

Press mixture against bottoms and sides of cups, leaving depression in the center.

Bake at 350° for 15 minutes. Remove from oven, break and drop an egg into each depression.

Bake 10 minutes longer or until are set to desired degree of firmness.

Serves 6.

NOTE: If this seems a bit too sweet for your taste, you can experiment by reducing the pineapple by half. It would then be wise to add more sour cream as the pineapple adds moisture to this dish.

Pancakes a la Norman

2 cups buttermilk (may substitute 2 cups sour milk)
2 tablespoons vinegar or lemon juice
2 cups milk minus 2 tablespoons
2 cups flour
3 teaspoons baking powder
1 teaspoon baking soda
1 tablespoon sugar
1 teaspoon salt
2 tablespoons butter or margarine
1 egg

Mix all dry ingredients. Mix butter and egg together. Combine two mixtures and blend

Cook on hot griddle or skillet that has been lightly buttered. Be sure pancake edges are dry and bubbles forming before turning over.

Serves 4-6.

Blintz Soufflé

This dish is more brunch than breakfast. It is very filling and rich and you should figure 1 to 1 1/2 blintzes per serving.

2 packages frozen cheese blintzes (6 per package)

DO NOT USE fruit-filled blintzes as soufflé will be too sweet. You may make your own blintzes for this dish, if you prefer.

1/4 pound margarine
1 1/2 cups sour cream
4 eggs
1/2 teaspoon vanilla
1/4 teaspoon salt
1/4 cup sugar, less 1 teaspoon
1/4 scant cup orange juice

Melt margarine in an oblong, glass casserole.

Separate blintzes and lay seam side down in casserole. It is not necessary to defrost blintzes before baking.

Beat eggs.

Mix all remaining ingredients, adding sour cream last.

Blend with eggs and pour over blintzes.

Bake in preheated oven at 350° for 40–45 minutes. Sauce will puff up around blintzes so do not let it get too brown on top.

Serve immediately. Taste will not be affected if it sits, but do not keep in oven as it may dry out.

Left-overs should be refrigerated immediately. Use a few spoonfuls of milk when reheating (cover tightly to retain the moisture).

Serves 6–8.

HINT: This dish may be assembled 8–10 hours before baking. Refrigerate immediately. May also be frozen, then baked. I let it defrost slightly before baking.

Schimmel Cheese Coffee Cake

The Schimmel family owned a small chain of hotels in the Midwest. The four brothers were trained in Europe and the service at the hotels and the restaurants was the epitome of old-world elegance and charm.

This coffee cake was served in the Orleans Room at the Blackstone Hotel in Omaha only for brunch.

The cake is so rich it could be served as a dessert but I like it as a breakfast coffee cake. Because it is so sweet, you will want to serve small portions.

My special thanks to Mrs. Bernard Schimmel for her permission to include this recipe.

Pastry dough:

3 packages yeast
3/4 pound butter
1/2 cup water
1/2 cup sugar
3 eggs
3 cups flour
1/2 cup milk
2 teaspoons vanilla

Filling:

24 ounces cream cheese
1/2 cup sugar
2 egg yolks
1 cup raisins
1 teaspoon lemon juice and zest
2 teaspoon vanilla
3/4 cup powdered sugar
1 1/2 teaspoons milk

Dissolve yeast in warm water.

In a large bowl, cream sugar with 4 tablespoons butter. Add flour, yeast, eggs, milk and vanilla. Mix well with wooden spoon. If the dough is very sticky, add another 1/2 cup flour.

Roll dough on floured board. Place pieces of remaining butter on dough. Fold the corners toward the middle and roll again. Repeat rolling and folding four more times.

If dough becomes unworkable, refrigerate between rollings as dough works best when cool. Refrigerate when this process is completed.

Blend the cream cheese, sugar and egg yolk until creamy. Add raisins, lemon juice, lemon zest and vanilla, mixing well.

Grease a 9" round cake pan. Line the pan with rolled pastry, reserving enough pastry to make a lattice top.

Pour filling into shell and form the lattice top. Allow to rise for an hour in a warm place.

Bake at 350° for 25–30 minutes.

When cool, brush the top with powdered sugar and milk mixture to glaze.

Serves 16.

Daisy Wheel Chipped Beef

A neighbor served this at a New Year's Eve midnight breakfast and while simple to prepare, it is fancy enough for brunches or luncheons.

1 package dried beef
2 tablespoons butter
2 tablespoons flour
1 cup milk (or half and half if you desire richer mixture)
2 hard boiled eggs, sliced
1/2 cup mushrooms, fresh is best
Few drops Tabasco sauce
Salt and pepper to taste

Pour boiling water over shredded dried beef. Drain.

Sauté mushrooms, put aside.

Make white sauce by cooking flour and butter together until bubbly.

Remove from heat, add 1 cup milk (or half and half). Add seasonings. Cook over low heat until smooth, stirring constantly. Add mushrooms and beef.

Spoon over toast points or biscuits.

Garnish

With sharp knife, cut small notches in egg slices, mix cut-out pieces in with the white sauce. Center one wheel-shaped egg on each serving. May dust with paprika for a spot of color.

HINT: If liquid is warm or at least room temperature, the risk of having lumpy sauce is reduced.

Serves 4.

SOUPS

All Night Chicken Soup

My mother catered meals for film crews and one of the problems in a 12–14 hour day—and all night shoots—was that everyone needed an energy boost but usually were "all coffeed out." She initially used this recipe as a cold, first course. One bitter cold winter while working on a car repair shop movie set, the heat was turned off a great deal of the time because the sound system picked up the noise of the blowers. By the end of the first day's shoot the cast was miserable and the crew was chilled to the bone even though they were wearing coats.

The next day she brought the hot version of this soup to the set. It was before crock pots and was kept hot in a pre-warmed gallon thermos jug. Since then it has been used in every conceivable location and the crew always asks for it.

Also delicious icy cold but the secret is that it must be cooked first, otherwise the flavors do not blend properly and the soup could have a greasy taste.

6 cans cream of chicken soup (15 to 16 ounces)
6 soup cans filled with the following depending on how rich you want the stock:
  3 with water and 3 with milk
OR 3 with milk or cream and 3 with chicken broth (can use chicken boullion cubes)
Add 1 teaspoon curry powder (up to 1 tablespoon if you like curry)
1 teaspoon plain mustard
Add salt to taste after above has simmered and flavors blended. Heat thoroughly but do not boil.

Garnishes

Minced parsley, slivered almonds, shredded chicken

HINT: Save money by using powdered cream or milk and dilute with enough water or chicken broth to equal liquid required. Keeps well in crock pot set at low.

Serves 6 generous servings.

Cucumber Chillers

To 6 cups basic cream soup stock add:

#1

1 cup diced cucumbers, well drained
Salt and pepper to taste
1/2 teaspoon lemon juice
Dash onion salt

Simmer until tastes blend, chill. Serves 6.

Garnish

Cucumber twists, mint or dill leaves

#2

2 cans (10 1/4 ounce) condensed cream of celery soup
1 cup milk
1 cup diced, drained cucumber
Dash Tabasco
1 cup sour cream

Combine in electric blender or whip by hand all ingredients except sour cream. Mixture will be thick. Mix in sour cream and chill for at least three hours. If too thick for your taste, blend in more milk. Serves 6.

Garnish

Dollop of sour cream on top, minced chives, sliver of pimento.

#3

2 cans (10 1/4 ounce) cream of potato soup
1 soup can water
1/2 cup sour cream
1/2 cup finely chopped cucumber

Follow directions for soup #2. Serves 6.

Whipped cream garnishes

To 1/4 cup heavy cream, whipped, add: 1/2 teaspoon prepared horseradish or 1 teaspoon grated lime rind or 1/2 teaspoon dill.

Soup on the Rocks

Fill glass with ice cubes, pour beef broth right from the can, over the cubes.

Garnish

Slice or wedge of lime or lemon.

Vichyssoise

2 cans (10 1/4 ounce) cream of potato soup
1 soup can milk—if you wish a richer broth, use half milk and half cream or add 2–4 tablespoons powdered cream to liquid.
1/4 teaspoon onion salt

Heat until blended. Chill at least three hours. Whip with blender or electric mixer for light and frothy texture.

Garnish

Minced parsley or slivers of chive tops.

Serves 6.

Chilled Avocado Soup

1 can (13 ounce) chicken broth
2 medium avocadoes, cut into chunks
2 tablespoons dry sherry
1/2 teaspoon salt
3/4 cup half and half
1/4 teaspoon onion powder
1/4 teaspoon dill weed
4 ounces sour cream (optional)

Put all ingredients except half & half into a blender and purée until smooth. Stir in half and half. Cover and chill for at least 2 hours. Serve with a dollop of sour cream on the top.

Serves 6.

Cold Black Bean Soup

   3 cans drained black beans
   6 tomatoes, chopped
   1 bunch cilantro or parsley
     (either will work and will cut the strong bean flavor)
   1 scallion, sliced

Combine and chill.

Sauce

   2 cups sour cream
   1 cup whipping cream
   1 teaspoon lime juice

Mix in glass bowl and chill at least two hours.

Serve in soup bowl, then top with the sauce. If you want more garnish than just the cream mixture, sprinkle chopped black olives on top.

Serves 4-6.

Chilled Tomato Soup

   6 tomatoes, quartered
   4 green onions, chopped
   2 tablespoons lemon juice
   1 teaspoon honey
   1 teaspoon basil
   1 teaspoon dill
   1 cup chicken broth
   Salt and pepper to taste

Purée the tomatoes and onions in a blender or food processor. Combine with rest of ingredients in a saucepan. Bring the soup to a boil. Turn off heat and allow soup to cool. Add more seasonings if desired and chill. Serve very cold, garnished with croutons or a dollop of sour cream.

Serves 4.

Spicy Gazpacho

3 cups spicy vegetable juice cocktail
1 green pepper, chopped
1 red pepper, chopped
1 cucumber, halved, seeded and chopped
1 onion, chopped
1 clove garlic, minced
1 1/2 tablespoons Worcestershire sauce
1/4 cup vegetable oil
1/4 cup wine vinegar
4 green onions, chopped
1 tomato, diced
Salt and pepper to taste
1 cup croutons (optional)

Purée juice, peppers, half of the cucumber, onion, garlic, Worcestershire and salt in a blender or food processor until smooth. Stir in oil and vinegar. Chill well. Garnish with the green onions, tomato and remaining cucumber. Top with croutons.

Serves 4–6.

Salmon Bisque

3/4 pound of poached salmon or 13 ounce can salmon, drained
1 onion, chopped
1 small green pepper, chopped
1 clove garlic, minced
1 tablespoon butter or margarine
2 teaspoons dill
2 1/2 cups milk or half and half
1/2 teaspoon Worcestershire sauce
2 tablespoons dry sherry or white wine
1 tablespoon lemon juice
Salt and pepper to taste

Sauté onion, garlic and pepper in margarine about 5 minutes. Put the onion mixture, salmon, milk, Worcestershire, dill, salt and pepper in a blender or processor and purée until smooth. Add the sherry or wine and lemon juice and blend well. Chill before serving.

Serves 4.

Taco Soup

1/2 pound beef stew meat or ground beef
1/4 cup onion, chopped
1 1/2 cups water
8 ounces tomato sauce
1 can (16 ounce) kidney beans, drained
1/2 envelope of powdered taco sauce
1 can (16 ounce) of stewed tomatoes, chopped

If you use stew meat, sauté until tender, adding the onions during the last 5 minutes of cooking. If you use ground beef, sauté the beef and onions together until well cooked. Drain off any grease. Add all the ingredients in a large saucepan and simmer for 20 minutes.

Serve with: sour cream, chopped avocado, taco chips, green onions, and grated cheddar cheese.

Serves 4.

Carrot Soup

3 tablespoons butter or margarine
8 carrots, chopped
1 onion, chopped
4 stalks celery, chopped
3 3/4 cups of chicken stock
1 cup of water
2 chicken bouillon cubes
Salt and pepper to taste
1/2 teaspoon dill or basil

In a large saucepan, melt margarine. Sauté carrots, onion and celery for 5 minutes. Add the stock, water and bouillon. Bring to a boil and then reduce heat and simmer for 10 minutes. Pour into a blender or food processor and purée. Return to simmer and add any necessary seasonings.

Garnish with chopped parsley or chives.

Serves 6.

Hot Black Bean Soup # 1

3 cans drained and rinsed black beans
10 strips chopped bacon, lightly cooked and drained
2 carrots, chopped
4 stalks celery, diced
2 cans or equivalent chicken stock (add more if too thick)
2–3 tablespoons tomato paste
Dash of garlic (optional)

Cook bacon, carrots and celery for about 4–5 minutes. Add beans and chicken stock. Simmer.

Thicken with tomato paste.

Serves 6.

Hot Black Bean Soup # 2

2 cans drained black beans
4–5 strips chopped bacon
2 tablespoons onions, chopped
1/8 teaspoon salt
1/8 teaspoon pepper
1/2 to 1 tablespoon cilantro or parsley, chopped
1 cup beer
2 cans or equivalent chicken stock (may need more)

Sauté bacon and onion. Be sure you have plenty of broth, adding chicken soup stock as needed. Serve in soup bowl or cup, garnish with 1 ounce grated Monterey Jack cheese.

Serves 6.

Black Bean Soup with Rice

1 pound black beans
1 chopped green pepper
1 chopped onion
1 chopped clove garlic
1/3 cup olive oil
2 cups cooked rice

After thoroughly washing the beans, cook in 2 quarts water with pepper, garlic and onion. Bring to a full boil, cover and reduce heat. Simmer until thickened and beans are tender.

Divide rice into 4–6 bowls. Ladle soup over rice.

Humpback whales average 40–60 feet in length and can weigh more than 40 tons.

Chinese Catch All Soup

I suspect this started out as a simple Won Ton soup and the chef just threw in all the food that was left on the counter—at least that's what I do. Again, it can start the meal or work as a light main course.

8 cups chicken broth (can use beef but it has a stronger flavor)
2 packages won tons cooked according to directions
1/2 cup cooked, shredded chicken
2–3 cups Chinese soft noodles (rice noodles) cooked
1/2 cup shrimp
1/2 cup peas, frozen or fresh, cooked
1/2 cup snow peas

Garnish

Sprinkle chives and slivers of carrots on top before serving

Use big bowls as this serves six generously.

Creamed Chicken Vegetable Soup

4 cans cream of chicken soup
3 soup cans milk, cream or chicken broth
2 packages (10 ounce) frozen mixed vegetables
1/4 teaspoon curry powder

Simmer all ingredients over low heat until vegetables are fully cooked.

If you want to serve this as a light meal, add one or two cups shredded chicken or turkey.

Serves 8.

Soup Combinations

One of the most versatile items you can stock is condensed soup—the thick, stick to-the-ribs types of soup.

Soups that can be combined for hearty main courses:

Cream of Chicken—Vegetable
Cream of Mushroom—Chicken with Rice
Beef Noodle—Vegetable
Cream of Celery—Vegetable, Cream of Chicken
Green Pea—Scotch Broth

HINT: A good way to make soup extra thick is to add instant mashed potatoes— a half cup or more to taste.

These combinations are the perfect place to use leftover meats or vegetables.

Goulash Soup

4 teaspoons paprika
1/2 cup chopped green pepper
10 tablespoons butter or margarine
5 cans condensed tomato soup (10–1/2 ounce)
5 soup cans of water
5 cups cubed cooked beef
1 teaspoon caraway seeds
1 teaspoon onion salt (optional)

Cook pepper and paprika until pepper is tender. Add and heat remaining ingredients over low heat. Stir often. Heat at least 5–10 minutes to let flavors mix.

May be served over noodles.

Serves 8–10.

French Onion Soup

An old favorite for any meal or a midnight snack.

2 cans condensed onion soup (10–1/2 ounce)
2 soup cans of water only 3/4 full
4–6 slices French bread
Butter
Parmesan cheese
Grated mozzarella, white cheddar or Swiss cheese for garnish

Simmer soup and water while buttering bread.

Arrange bread on cookie sheet, sprinkle with Parmesan cheese and broil until very lightly browned.

Pour soup into oven-proof individual bowls, crocks, or soup tureen.

Serves 4–6.

Japanese Noodle Soup

One of the things I love about my job is the opportunity to learn to cook dishes from all over the world. Hawaii gives new meaning to the word "melting pot" when it comes to the variety of cultures that live and cook there.

While some of these ingredients sound exotic, you'll be surprised to find that most large supermarkets carry them. Also, even medium-sized cities often have a market carrying Asian or Oriental foods.

Zaru Soba (cold buckwheat noodles)

Cook soba as directed on package. Drain, rinse with cold water and drain again. Chill for at least 30 minutes.

Make 2 packages of basic Japanese soup stock according to package directions. Add noodles and sprinkle with slivers of green onion.

Serves 4.

Cheese Soup with Beer

This is a very robust version of cheese soup due to the beer.

- **2 cups milk**
- **2 cups dark beer**
- **16 ounces cheese spread or melted cheese (cheddar or colby)**
- **1/2 cup flour**
- **1/4 cup melted margarine**
- **1/4 teaspoon salt**
- **1/8 teaspoon nutmeg (optional)**
- **1–2 ounces bacon bits (optional)**

Mix beer, milk and melted cheese in a pan and warm. Combine flour and melted margarine and form into a ball. Add the ball to the warm liquid. Mix thoroughly then cook over low heat stirring constantly until ball dissolves and the soup has thickened. Stir in bacon and salt.

Garnishes

Popcorn, extra bacon bits, croutons.

Makes 6 cups.

Sitka Soups

In 1804 Alexander Baranof established a settlement on the site of an old Tlingit village. This became, and remained the capitol of Russian America until it was purchased by the United States in October of 1867.

The area around Sitka is rich in history and customs from that period. The Sitka National Historical Park is a rare treat, history-wise. In 1804 a battle was fought there between the Tlingit Indians and the Russian troops. The fort and battle site have been interpreted and preserved. The Visitor Center houses artifacts, exhibits and craft workshops. However, most visitors feel the crowning glory of the park is the path leading to the fort; it is lined with eighteen fine totem poles. A quiet stroll through the area, especially on a misty day, makes one feel as if they had returned via a time machine.

In 1966, a fire damaged St. Michael's Cathedral, the famous Russian Orthodox church whose onion-shaped dome shining high above main street symbolizes Sitka to the outside world. The church has been restored and fortunately it's many beautiful artifacts and priceless treasures, including icons, were saved. The current Cathedral is an exact replica of the original, and was rebuilt on the same site.

The Sitka Russian Folk Dancers formed a group to offer visitors a chance to savor the town's Russian heritage. The Russian Bishop of that time helped translate information from a book of dances and assisted in teaching a few simple folk dances. Though amateurs by definition, they have had professional guidance from instructors of Russian dance.

The heritage of old Russia shows itself in many of the recipes that have been handed down through the generations.

Russian Sauerkraut Soup

1 pound beef short ribs
1 pound soup bones
3/4–1 cup onions, chopped
1 cup carrots, chopped
3/4–1 cup celery, chopped
4 cups coarsely chopped cabbage
1/2 teaspoon garlic salt
1 1/2 quarts of water
14 ounces canned tomatoes
2 bay leaves
1/4 teaspoon pepper
1/8 cup lemon juice
1 tablespoon sugar
8 ounces canned sauerkraut, rinsed and well drained

Roast short ribs and bones in a 450° oven for about 20 minutes. Turn once.

Put water in large soup kettle, then add ribs and bones. Add all but last three ingredients. Bring to a boil, then skim off foam.

Reduce heat. Cover and simmer for about 1-1/2 to 2 hours. Skim if necessary. When done, remove and discard soup bones. If meat has not fallen off the bone, you may cube it and return to pot.

Add the lemon juice, sugar and sauerkraut. Again, heat to boil, then reduce and simmer for one hour, covered.

Makes approximately two quarts.

Serves 8.

Borscht (Beet Soup)

There are many complicated recipes for borscht, but this one is fast and easy.

2 cans beets
1–1 1/2 cans of water
1 beef boullion cube
1–2 tablespoons lemon juice (to taste)
1–2 teaspoons sugar or artificial sweetener.
1/2 cup sour cream

Purée beets in a blender using juice from the can.

Dissolve boullion cube in **1 cup water**—do not add rest of water yet.

Add water, lemon juice and sugar to beet mixture. Simmer on low fire to blend flavors.

Chill at least two hours. Taste. At this point you may wish to add more water and additional lemon juice for tartness.

NOTE: When you mix sour cream into the soup, it cuts the tartness and actually sweetens the soup.

May be served in soup bowl or mug. Garnish with spoonful of sour cream. For added color, sprinkle minced chives on top.

Serves 4.

Cream of Pumpkin Soup

1/2 cup chopped onions
3 tablespoons margarine or butter
2 cans pumpkin (29 ounces)
  or 4 pounds fresh peeled and cubed pumpkin
1 small bay leaf
1 teaspoon dried thyme
3 cups half and half or dairy creamer
5–8 cups chicken broth
1/4 teaspoon of curry powder (optional)

Fresh pumpkin: Using a large kettle, sauté onions in margarine until soft. Add 8 cups chicken broth, pumpkin, bay leaf and thyme.

Cover. Simmer 15–20 minutes until pumpkin is soft enough to put in blender.

Canned pumpkin: Using **only** five cups of chicken broth, repeat as for fresh pumpkin.

Remove bay leaf, and put pumpkin through a sieve, or use blender or food processor.

Cool. Stir in half and half and simmer for five minutes. Add salt and pepper to taste.

Soup can be served hot or cold.

Garnishes

Spoonful of whipped, unsweetened cream on top. Sprinkle on minced parsley or green onion tops.

Serves 10–12.

Easy Chili

Everyone has a good recipe for chili. The reason I like this one is that it is quick and easy to make.

- 1/2–1 cup water
- 1 can (15 ounce) tomato sauce
- 1 can whole tomatoes, chopped
- 1 can (28 ounce) stewed tomatoes, process or put through blender for about 10 seconds
- 1 pound hamburger, cooked
- 1 large green pepper, chopped
- 1 large onion, chopped
- Chili powder salt, pepper, onion powder and cumin to taste

Place all ingredients in a large pot. Mix well, bring to a boil and immediately lower heat, simmer for at least 1 hour.

If you like very spicy chili you may add a diced jalapeno pepper or Tabasco sauce.

Serves 4.

Alvin's Super Hardy Chili

Nothing hits the spot like a good, thick chili, especially on a cold day. My dad is a great one for poking through the cupboards to find something to "add" to whatever he's making. This chili/roast beef hash combination is a great one dish informal main course as well as a good luncheon choice.

- 3–4 cans chili without beans
- 2 cans roast beef hash
- 1 teaspoon Heinz 57 sauce
- 1 tablespoon minced onion (optional)
- Grated American cheese

Heat thoroughly, then garnish with grated American cheese before serving.

Serves 4.

SALADS

Herb Marinated Tomatoes

1/3 cup vegetable oil
2 tablespoons wine vinegar
1/2 teaspoon tarragon
1/2 teaspoon basil
1/2 teaspoon salt (optional)
dash of ground pepper
3 large tomatoes, sliced

Combine first six ingredients and whisk until well blended. Put tomatoes in a shallow bowl. Pour dressing over tomatoes and chill for 2–3 hours. Drain.

You can use any combination of herbs you like, these just happen to be two of my favorites.

Confetti Cottage Cheese

1 carton (16 ounce) small-curd, creamy cottage cheese
1/3 cup green pepper, chopped
2 tablespoons green onion, chopped
1/3 cup red pepper, chopped or pimento, chopped
2 teaspoons prepared horseradish (optional)

Combine all ingredients and chill.

This makes a very colorful alternative to regular salad. Great for dieters.

Hot Tomato Salad

This is another dish I made in Sydney. It too makes interesting use of an everyday vegetable.

> 1 pound firm tomatoes
> 2 onions, chopped
> 1 tablespoon oil
> 1 tablespoon chopped fresh basil
>   Or 1/2 teaspoon dried basil
> 3 shallots
> salt (optional)

Peel tomatoes, chop coarsely.

Heat oil in pan, add onions and cook until transparent. Add tomatoes, stir over medium heat until heated thoroughly but don't overcook or it could turn mushy on you.

Remove from heat, stir in basil and shallots, add salt.

Sliced Cucumbers in Sour Cream or Yogurt

> 1 large cucumber, sliced thin
> 1 cup plain nonfat yogurt OR 1 cup sour cream
> 1 tablespoon mint, chopped
> 1/2 teaspoon garlic, minced
> 1/2 teaspoon salt (optional)

Mix all ingredients and pour over cucumbers. Chill for several hours before serving.

Serves 4–6

Makes an excellent accompaniment to curries.

Coleslaw

1 small head green cabbage
1 small head red cabbage
1 small onion, chopped
1/2 cup vegetable oil
3/4 cup sugar
3/4 cup white or cider vinegar
1 teaspoon celery salt
1 tablespoon dry mustard
1/2 cup golden raisins (optional)

Shred cabbage and stir in onion. Mix the rest of the ingredients together and toss with cabbage. Chill for at least 1 hour.

Spinach Coleslaw

1/4 head of cabbage
1 small bunch spinach
2 medium onions
1 small red pepper, seeded
1 small green pepper, seeded
2 medium carrots
1 teaspoon sugar
Salt and pepper
1/2 cup French dressing

I found this recipe when I was living in Australia and I think it makes a nice change of pace from ordinary coleslaw.

Wash cabbage and spinach, drain well. Shred cabbage and spinach. Cut peeled onions in half, then slice thin. Finely slice red and green peppers, and carrots. Toss together and refrigerate.

Mix rest of ingredients, chill until ready to serve.

3–Bean Salad

3/4–1 cup thick salsa
1/4 cup salad oil
1–1/2 teaspoons chili powder
1 teaspoon salt (optional)
1 can (16 ounce) black beans, drained
1 can (15–20 ounce) kidney beans, drained
1 can (15–20 ounce) garbanzo beans, drained
3 celery stalks, sliced
1 small red onion, chopped
1 tomato, diced
Juice of 2 small limes

In large bowl, mix salsa, oil, chili powder, salt, and lime juice. Add rest of ingredients, toss to mix.

Cover and chill for at least 30–60 minutes. Can be made a day ahead of time.

Serves 8.

Marinated Green Beans

1 pound of fresh green beans OR
1 pound can whole green beans, drained
1/4 cup bottled OR homemade Italian style salad dressing

If using fresh green beans, blanch in boiling water for about 2 minutes, until they turn bright green, but remain very crisp. Marinate beans in the dressing for 2–3 hours in the refrigerator.

To serve, drain and either serve with sliced tomatoes, in a salad or try wrapping a bundle of the beans in thinly sliced cold cuts.

Black Bean Salad

Drain canned black beans. Add chopped green pepper and onions in amount geared to your personal taste. Check before adding seasoning as these beans will be fairly salty. Mix well and chill for several hours. You can add fresh, chopped tomatoes. This can be marinated in Italian or vinaigrette dressing.

Dill Cucumber–Pasta Salad

1 small onion, chopped
2 medium cucumbers
1/2 cup plain yogurt
2 green onions, chopped
2–3 tablespoons fresh dill, finely chopped
1/8 teaspoon dry mustard
1 tablespoon white vinegar
1 tablespoon vegetable oil
8 ounces pasta shells or twists, cooked just until tender

Peel cucumbers, cut in half lengthwise and slice fairly thin. Place in a strainer or colander, cover with a saucer and weight down to help press the water out of the cucumbers. Leave to drain for at least 1 hour.

Combine yogurt, dill, mustard, vinegar and oil, blend well. Add salt and pepper to taste. Combine cucumbers, onions and pasta. Add dressing, sparingly and toss to mix. Chill for 1 hour.

Serves 6.

Zucchini and Potato Salad

Almost everyone loves potato salad and there must be as many recipes as there is sand on the beach but this one really has a different flavor.

6 medium-sized red potatoes
3 small zucchini
1/2 small red onion, chopped
2 red peppers OR 1 red and 1 yellow, cut into bite size pieces
1/3 cup fresh basil, chopped coarsely
1 tablespoon oil
1/2 cup mayonnaise OR 1/2 cup plain yogurt
3 tablespoons cider vinegar
2 tablespoons milk
Salt and pepper to taste

In a large saucepan place unpeeled potatoes. Fill with just enough water to cover. Bring to a boil, reduce heat, cover and simmer for about 20–25 minutes or until potatoes are just tender.

Drain, cool and cut into bite size pieces.

Cut zucchini into bite size pieces. Heat oil in a skillet and stir-fry zucchini for about 2 minutes or until crisp and bright green. Cool.

In large bowl, mix mayonnaise or yogurt, vinegar, milk and salt and pepper. Add zucchini, potatoes, onion, peppers and basil. Gently toss with dressing, coating all ingredients well. Cover and chill for at least 2 hours.

Serves 6–8.

Spinach Pasta Salad

16 ounces spinach pasta
1 cup sweet pickles, chopped
2 green onions, chopped
1/2 cup sour cream
1 1/2 cups mayonnaise
2 tomatoes, chopped
2 tablespoons dill weed
1 tablespoon sweet pickle juice
1/4 cup milk
Salt and pepper to taste

Cook pasta according to package directions, until tender. Rinse with cold water and drain. Place noodles in a large bowl and moisten with milk. Combine sour cream and mayonnaise and whisk until creamy. Add the dill, pickle juice, salt and pepper and mix well. Pour over noodles. Add the green onions, tomatoes, and pickles. Mix well and chill.

Serves 10.

Marinated Carrots

2 pounds carrots, sliced fairly thick
2/3 cup cider vinegar
1/2 cup vegetable oil
1/2 cup sugar
1 small onion, sliced thinly
1 package Italian salad dressing mix
1/4 cup fresh parsley, chopped

Blanch carrots **very** slightly, no more then 1 minute. Mix all the rest of the ingredients, except the onions. Place carrots and onions in a bowl and pour the mixture over them. Let marinate in refrigerator for at least 3–4 hours, overnight is even better.

Serves 6–8.

Cool Cucumber Salad

Even people who don't care for cucumbers rave about this mold. The cucumber flavor is subtle and this mixture is just tart enough to enhance almost any main dish.

1 package (3 ounce) lime gelatin
3/4 cup hot water
1/4 cup lemon juice
1/2 teaspoon onion juice or 1/4 teaspoon onion salt
1 cup sour cream OR mayonnaise
    or make it half of each
1 cup cucumber, peeled, chopped, and well drained

Dissolve gelatin in boiling hot water. Add lemon juice and onion flavoring. Chill until partially set. Fold in cream and cucumbers. If you can't wait for it to partially set, you may want to occasionally stir mixture while it is becoming firm to prevent cucumbers from raising to the top of the mold. Although if they do, it gives you a darker green strip on the bottom which does look pretty when unmolded. I like to put this in a round mold and fill the center with baby tomatoes or olives. You can also use a loaf-shaped pan, then slice it and serve on bed of lettuce with a dollop of sour cream on top.

Most of what we know about whales are "guesstimates" as we are studying them as they roam the oceans.

Dressings

Dijon Dressing

> 1/4 cup olive oil
> 1/4 cup white wine
> 1/2 cup half and half
> 2 tablespoons Dijon mustard
> 1 clove garlic, minced or to taste
> Paprika, salt and pepper to taste

Place all ingredients in a blender or a bowl and blend or whisk until very well mixed.

Makes about 1 cup.

Dijon-Honey Dressing

> 1 cup oil
> 2 tablespoons Dijon mustard
> 1/2 cup honey
> 1/4 cup white wine vinegar
> 3/4 cup mayonnaise
> 1/3 cup parsley, chopped
> 1 tablespoon onion, chopped
> 1 tablespoon celery seed
> 1 tablespoon mint, chopped

Place all ingredients in blender or a bowl. Blend or whisk until very well mixed. Chill.

Makes about 2 3/4 cups.

Dijon-Dill Dressing

1/2 cup mayonnaise
1 tablespoon tarragon vinegar
1 tablespoon Dijon mustard
1 tablespoon olive oil
pepper to taste
1 teaspoon dill

Place all ingredients in blender or a bowl. Blend or whisk until very well mixed. Chill.

Makes about 3/4 cup.

Balsamic Vinegar Dressing

1/4 cup olive oil, preferably extra-virgin
1/4 cup vegetable oil
1 1/2 ounces red-wine vinegar
1/2 ounces balsamic vinegar
Salt and pepper to taste

Combine all ingredients. Whisk for several minutes, until slightly thickened.

Sweet Italian Dressing

1 cup vegetable oil
1/3 cup cider vinegar
1/4 cup sugar
1 clove garlic, minced or to taste
1 teaspoon salt

Combine all ingredients. Whisk until well blended. Chill for at least 1 hour.

Dressing for Fruit Salad

1 cup mayonnaise
1 cup crushed strawberries
1 cup finely chopped cranberries
2 tablespoons raspberry puree
1 tablespoon powdered sugar
1 teaspoon orange juice

Mix strawberries with 1 tablespoon powdered sugar.

Mix cranberries with a teaspoon of orange juice. Mix all together and chill before serving.

Macaroni Fruit Salad

This is another dish that sounds like a strange combination. The variety of the fruit textures blending with the macaroni creates an interesting change of pace flavor.

1 cup macaroni, cooked
Mayonnaise to moisten only
1 tablespoon sliced or diced peaches
1 teaspoon raisins
1 tablespoon sliced or diced nectarines
1 tablespoon pears
1 tablespoon apricots
1 tablespoon diced celery

Blend thoroughly and chill before serving.

Yield 1 1/2 cups.

Fruits with Creamy Fruit-based Dip

1/2 cup mayonnaise-style salad dressing
2 tablespoons peach, apricot, pineapple or raspberry preserves
1 cup frozen whipped topping, thawed

Combine salad dressing and preserves, mixing well.

Fold in whipped topping and serve as a dip for assorted fruits that have been cut into cubes or spears.

A drained, scooped out pineapple is good for serving the dip.

A very large, well drained orange or grapefruit works well.

If you can get a fresh coconut and slice off the top, you'll have a fun serving dish but you will need to support the pointy bottom. A piece of styrofoam works for that purpose, and if you cover it with leaves or flowers you have the focal point for a decorative center piece. In Hawaii we are blessed with cheap access to the beautiful, glossy Ti leaves. They are used to decorate everything from the food to the tables. Many florists on the mainland now carry Ti leaves.

On a trip to Bora Bora my parents were even served their food on Ti leaves. They are sturdy and safe to use as plates and can now be purchased at most florists.

FISH
AND SEAFOOD

It's easy to get spoiled when you live on the ocean. Working from Alaska south to Washington State and west to Hawaii, I've had a chance to make some delightful fish dishes.

I've also encountered some challenging situations. My months of cooking on the converted trawler presented me with intriguing Alaskan escapades. Hunks of glacier ice were used for refrigeration purposes.

Pieces "calve" or break loose from the main flow while slabs of various sizes float through the bay. We simply captured whatever we needed to fill our ice chests.

Spicy Fish, Indian Style

2 pounds any firm fleshed fish
1 tablespoon sugar
1/2 teaspoon red pepper flakes
1 teaspoon garlic powder
1/2 teaspoon cumin
1/2 teaspoon powdered coriander seed
3 tablespoons white vinegar
2 onions, chopped
16 ounce can tomato sauce

Mix all of above except onions and tomato sauce.

Cube fish and marinate in this mixture for 1 hour.

Sauté onions in butter or margarine until brown. Add tomato sauce and simmer for 10 minutes. Add fish and marinade, cook 10–15 minutes. Serve with rice.

Serves 4.

Artichoke and Crab Casserole

1/2 cup butter or margarine
1 small onion, minced
1/2 cup flour
4 cups cream
   OR 2 cups half and half and 2 cups milk
1/2 cup Madeira or dry sherry
2 tablespoons lemon juice
3–4 cups crabmeat, imitation or the real thing
2–2 1/2 cups artichoke hearts, coarsely chopped (not marinated)
3 cups shell macaroni, cooked and drained
2 cups grated Swiss or Gruyère cheese
Paprika

Preheat oven to 350°. Melt butter or margarine in a large pan. (You may substitute a large electric frying pan.)

Add onion, sauté until golden. Stir in flour, cook over low heat until flour is pale yellow. Remove from heat. Add cream, stir or whisk vigorously.

Return to medium heat and stir until sauce comes to a boil. Reduce heat and add Madeira or sherry.

Season to taste with salt and pepper.

Pour lemon juice over crabmeat and toss lightly.

Combine crab, artichokes, and macaroni. Mix into sauce.

Pour into buttered 6 quart casserole. Sprinkle with paprika. Bake until heated through, about 25–30 minutes. Be careful not to overcook or sauce may dry out.

Serves 10–12.

May be made 1 day before, refrigerated and brought to room temperature before baking.

You may substitute cooked chicken for the crab.

Tuna Stroganoff

1/2 cup onion, minced or 4 green onions
1 medium clove garlic, minced (optional)
2 tablespoons butter or margarine
1 can cream of mushroom soup
2/3 cup sour cream
1/3 cup milk
Juice of 1/2 lemon
14 ounces tuna, drained and flaked
1/2–3/4 cup mushrooms, sliced
Cooked rice or noodles
Paprika

Sauté onions and garlic in butter or margarine in skillet until tender. Add soup, milk, sour cream, lemon juice and pepper to taste. Stir in tuna and mushrooms. Heat thoroughly.

Serve over noodles or rice. Dust with paprika.

Serves 4.

Cream Cheese Stuffed Salmon Steaks

6 salmon steaks, one inch thick
4 ounces cream cheese
2 tablespoons grated Parmesan cheese
1 tablespoon each: chopped parsley, chopped basil and chopped
green onion
3 tablespoons margarine, melted
2 tablespoons lemon juice
Salt and pepper to taste

Rinse salmon and pat dry.

Through the round part of each steak, make a cut to the center bone, creating a pocket. Combine cheeses, parsley, basil and green onions, blend well.

Divide into six portions. Roll each portion into a ball and flatten. Place one portion into the pocket of each steak. Fasten with toothpicks.

Place on well greased broiler pan. Combine margarine, lemon juice, salt and pepper. Baste salmon with margarine mixture.

Broil 4–5 inches from heat source for about 4–5 minutes. Turn. Baste and cook another 4–5 minutes, or until salmon flakes easily when tested with a fork.

Serves 6.

May substitute tuna, shark, sea bass or any other firm flesh fish.

Salmon Fettuccini

4 ounce can salmon
3 tablespoons butter or margarine
2 tablespoons green onions, chopped
1 cup cream or half and half
Juice of 1 lemon
12 ounces cooked, drained fettuccini

Melt butter in skillet. Add onions and cook until tender. Blend in cream and lemon juice. Add salmon and heat thoroughly. Add to pasta and toss well. Sprinkle with grated Parmesan cheese and paprika.

Serves 4.

May add 2 tablespoons chopped basil to sauce, if desired.

Pasta Alfredo with Smoked Salmon

The first time we tasted this combination was at Spagos, the gathering place of Hollywood stars on Sunset Strip. While this is not their recipe, I hope it will give you a wonderful new version to add to your pasta recipes.

8 ounces medium egg noodles
1/2 pint cream
1/2 cup melted margarine or butter
1/8 teaspoon salt
1/3 cup grated Parmesan cheese
1/4–1/2 cup shredded smoked salmon

Cook noodles, following package directions. Drain.

Mix cream, margarine and salt in a saucepan. Toss together with slivers of smoked salmon.

Dust top of dish with the cheese.

Makes 2 servings or 4 appetizer-size servings.

Garnish

Minced chives, tiny capers or a sprinkle of black caviar.

Depression Salmon Loaf

When I was faced with cooking on budgets that often allowed me to spend only $4–5 a day per person, I really had to hunt for recipes.

During the depression, my grandmother Mabel went to work before 8 am, worked all day, then had to come home at night and make dinner. She not only looked for ways to stretch the dollar, but for meals she could prepare in the morning, refrigerate and cook in the evening. The capers are a luxury she never would have dreamed of using in those days. While they are fairly expensive, one bottle can be used for a dozen meals or more, so it is still cost-effective to use them to add a new twist to an old standby.

> **1 large can salmon (red or pink) if using pink, add 2 tablespoons ketchup to mix, drain and reserve liquid**
> **1 tablespoon lemon juice**
> **3 cups finely grated cracker crumbs or bread crumbs**
> **1/2 teaspoon celery salt**
> **1/2 teaspoon onion salt, or fresh grated onion**
> **2 eggs, beaten**
> **1 teaspoon capers**
> **Dill weed for garnish**

Drain salmon, reserving liquid. Mash with bones (great source of calcium) until almost a paste.

Beat eggs. Add crumbs to eggs, stir well. Blend in rest of ingredients, mix well. Add liquid from the can until mixture is thoroughly moistened (up to about 1/2 can) but not runny.

Bake in greased loaf pan for 45 minutes at 350° or until set. Loaf should be firm in the center (test with knife as you would a soufflé). Unmold on warmed platter, ladle on cream sauce and garnish with sprinkle of dill weed.

A simple cream sauce goes nicely with this. If you want something a bit more tangy, add about 1 tablespoon of lemon juice to the sauce.

Serves 4–6.

Grilled Shark, Mexican Style

1 1/2 pounds shark
1/3 cup lime juice
3 cloves garlic, minced
2 tablespoons vegetable oil
1/3 cup beer
2 teaspoons chopped parsley
1/2–1 teaspoon cumin
2 teaspoons dijon mustard
Salt and pepper to taste
12 ounces salsa
1 ripe avocado

Rinse fish, pat dry and set aside.

Combine all ingredients except salsa and pour over fish. Marinate in refrigerator at least 1 hour, turning once.

When ready to grill, drain marinade and reserve. Place under broiler or on a greased barbecue 4–5 inches from coals.

Cook about 4–5 minutes, baste with marinade and turn. Cook another 4–5 minutes, or until fish flakes when tested with fork.

Serve with salsa and sliced avocado.

Serves 4.

Use any firm fleshed fish (tuna, sea bass, halibut).

Grilled Shark Teriyaki

1 1/2 pounds shark steaks
20 ounce can pineapple chunks
3 tablespoons soy sauce preferably salt reduced
2 tablespoons sherry or white wine
1 tablespoon ginger root, finely grated
1/2 teaspoon dry mustard
2 cloves garlic, minced
2 teaspoons brown sugar
2 green peppers, cut into large pieces
    (if available use red or yellow peppers
    along with the green one)
1–2 onions, cut into large chunks

Rinse shark and dry. Set aside.

Drain pineapple, reserve 3 tablespoons of juice, set pineapple aside. Make marinade with reserve pineapple juice, soy sauce, sherry, ginger mustard, garlic and brown sugar.

Mix well and pour over shark. Marinate in refrigerator for at least 1 hour, turning once.

Use metal or bamboo skewers and make kabobs alternating pineapple, green peppers, and onions, set aside.

Drain shark, reserving marinade. Place on well greased barbecue grill 4–5 inches from coals, or on a broiler rack in oven.

Cook 4–5 minutes, baste with marinade and turn.

Cook another 4–5 minutes or until shark flakes when tested with fork. Baste kabobs with marinade and place on grill for about 45–60 seconds on each side or until just brown.

Serves 4.

Grilled Whole Salmon

1 whole salmon, cleaned
Fresh or dry dill weed, to taste
Lemon pepper to taste
1/2–3/4 cup lemon juice
1 lemon, sliced
3/4 cup white wine or water

Rinse fish and pat dry.

Cut 3 or 4 shallow diagonal slashes into each side of salmon.

Combine dill and lemon pepper and rub inside fish and into the slashes. Place slices of lemon inside fish.

Place fish in a foil lined pan. Combine the wine (or water) and lemon juice and place in same pan with fish. Seal foil around fish, so no steam escapes.

Bake at 325° allowing approximately 10 minutes per inch of salmon measured at its thickest part.

Fish is done when it flakes easily when tested with a fork.

Allow 3/4–1 pound of fish per person.

Grilled Fish

Brush the grill and the fish with oil so it will not stick to the grill. Baste frequently will cooking. Fish should be 4–6 inches away from the heat.

If making kabobs, use square-sided or flat skewers, not round.

If using several types of fish and vegetables that cook for a different length of time, put on separate skewers.

Salmon Cheese Cake

1 cup white bread crumbs
15 1/2 ounce can, pink or red salmon or tuna, drained
12 ounces cream
8 ounces cream cheese
2 eggs
1/2 cup mayonnaise
1 cup cheddar cheese, grated
4 green onions, chopped
1/2 teaspoon dill

Press bread crumbs over base of greased 8" or 9" springform pan. Flake fish with a fork, stir in 1/4 cup of the cream, press gently over bread crumb base. Beat cream cheese in small bowl with electric mixer until smooth. Beat in eggs, mayonnaise and remaining cream. Stir in cheese, green onions and dill. Pour over fish mixture. Place on cookie sheet, bake at 350° for one hour, 15 minutes or until set and lightly brown. Let stand 10 minutes before removing from pan and serving.

Serves 6.

Baked Herb Fish

2 pounds halibut or red snapper filets
1/2 cup butter or margarine
2/3 cup soda crackers, finely crushed
1/4 cup grated Parmesan cheese
1 teaspoon basil
1/4 teaspoon garlic powder
Lemon pepper (to taste)

Melt margarine in a 9" x 13" pan. Combine cracker crumbs, cheese, basil, garlic powder and lemon pepper. Dip fish in margarine then roll in cracker crumb mix. Put fish back into 9" x 13" pan. Bake at 350° for 25–30 minutes or until fish is tender and flakes easily with a fork.

Serves 4.

Easy Shrimp Curry

2 pounds shrimp, cleaned and deveined
1 can cream of shrimp soup
1 can cream of mushroom soup
1 1/2 cups milk
1 cup sour cream
1 teaspoon curry powder, or to taste
1 tablespoon parsley, chopped

Sauté shrimp in 1/4 pound butter or margarine until tender, about 4 minutes.

Mix all other ingredients together and add to shrimp. Heat through, without boiling.

Serve on bed of rice.

Serves 4.

Easy Baked Halibut

3 pounds halibut
1/4 cup celery, chopped
1 tablespoon parsley, chopped
1/4 cup onion, chopped
2 tablespoons fresh basil, shopped
1 can (10 ounce) cream of mushroom soup
1/2 cup milk

Combine all ingredients and pour over the halibut. Sprinkle with paprika. Cover and bake at 350° for 1 hour.

Serves 6.

Fish and Vegetables

3 tablespoons flour
3 tablespoons butter or margarine
2 onions, chopped
1 clove garlic, minced

In large skillet, brown butter and flour. Add onions and garlic, brown slightly. To this add the following and cook slowly for about 10 minutes:

1 teaspoon parsley, chopped
3 green onions, chopped
1 green or red pepper, chopped
2 stalks celery, chopped
1 can (15 ounce) of tomatoes
2 bay leaves
1 teaspoon Worcestershire sauce
1 small lemon, sliced
Dash of Tabasco
Salt and pepper to taste

Add: **4 pounds fish** (preferably a firm white fish)

Cover and simmer for 10 minutes. Turn fish and cook for 5 minutes.

Add 1/2 cup white wine and simmer until fish tests done.

Serves 8.

Crab Imperial

1 pound crab meat (may use imitation crab)
2 tablespoons butter or margarine
1 tablespoon flour
1/2 cup milk
1 teaspoon onion, minced
1 1/2 teaspoons Worcestershire sauce
2 slices white bread, crust removed and cubed
1/2 cup mayonnaise
Juice of 1/2 lemon

In large skillet, melt 1 tablespoon butter, add flour and blend well. Slowly add the milk. Stir constantly until sauce boils and thickens. Mix in onion, Worcestershire and bread cubes. Stir well then set aside to cool.

In a small bowl combine the mayonnaise, lemon juice, salt and pepper to taste. Set aside.

In another skillet melt and brown 1 tablespoon butter. Add crab and toss lightly. Mix all ingredients together and spoon into a greased 1 quart casserole. Sprinkle with paprika and bake at 450° for 10–15 minutes.

Serves 4.

Crab Cakes

2 cups flour
1 egg
1 pound crab (may use imitation crab)
1/2 teaspoon sugar
2 tablespoons oil
1/2 onion, minced (optional)
1/4 teaspoon minced parsley (optional)

Mix all but crab until well blended. Add crab. Form patties and chill for at least 30 minutes. Fry like pancakes.

Serves 4.

Cheesy Halibut Sticks

2 pounds halibut steaks, 1" thick
1 cup grated Parmesan or Romano cheese
1/2 cup oil
1/2 cup fine bread crumbs
1 clove minced garlic

Cut halibut into strips about 1" wide by 2" long. Combine oil, salt to taste and garlic. Marinate fish for 2 minutes, then drain. Roll in grated cheese, then roll in crumbs. Place on Teflon or lightly greased baking sheet so pieces don't touch. Bake in hot oven (450°) for about 12 minutes, until brown.

Serves 4.

Whale Songs—Humpbacks have very complex songs which may be similar in sound in different areas of the oceans. As far as we know, only the males sing—almost exclusively in breeding grounds. The songs change over a period of time and all whales change songs at the same time.

Sauces for Fish

Pimento Sauce

> 8 ounce carton sour cream
> Pimentoes
> Dill pickles
> Dijon mustard
> Basil
> Small onion, chopped

Purée everything together in blender. Spread on fish and bake. Works well as a sauce for any fish.

Super Easy Sauce
OR How to Avoid Dried Out Baked Fish

A lot of people have a difficult time keeping fish from drying out, especially if it is a thin fillet. This recipe was given to me by my friend, Diane, who is a native of the Bahamas.

> Mayonnaise (not salad dressing)
> Onion, sliced
> Tomatoes, sliced
> Dill

Place fish in foil-lined baking dish and spread mayonnaise over the top. Layer sliced onion and tomato on top of the mayonnaise. Sprinkle with dill. Seal foil and bake.

Amounts used and baking time will vary according to quantity of fish and thickness of cut.

Super Easy Sauce for Fish #1

Equal parts mayonnaise and horseradish
Juice of 1 lemon

Place fish in pan. Cover with sauce, sprinkle with paprika and broil until fish is tender and sauce is brown and bubbly.

Sauce for Fish #2

8 ounces sour cream
1 can whole pimentoes
1 whole dill pickle
1 tablespoon Dijon mustard
1 teaspoon basil
3 tablespoons chopped onion

Purée all ingredients in blender or processor. Spread on fish, cover and bake at 350° for about 25 minutes or until fish flakes easily with a fork.

Sauce for Fish #3

The first time I tried this sauce was at a salmon bake near Juneau. The salmon was cooked slowly outside over wood. You can duplicate the effect on your barbecue or even broil it in the oven.

Brown sugar
Lemon juice

Measure about three parts sugar to one part lemon juice. It should be like syrup. Baste fish and cook. Baste again when you turn it over.

Tuna–Cheese Soufflé

We grew up on this dish long before soufflés and quiches were considered "masculine" and my brother and father always loved it.

3 tablespoons butter or margarine
1/4 cup flour
1 cup milk
1 cup grated cheddar cheese (or longhorn)
1/4 teaspoon salt
1/4 teaspoon dry mustard
1/4 teaspoon oregano (optional)
6 eggs, separated
1 can (6 1/2–7 ounce) tuna

Melt butter in saucepan, blend in flour. Gradually stir in milk. Stir while cooking until sauce starts to boil. Add cheese and seasoning. Stir and heat until cheese has melted.

Beat egg yolks and gradually stir into cheese mixture. Add tuna.

Now, here's where we separate the men from the boys. The original recipe separates the eggs, beating the white until stiff but not dry, then gently folding into the mixture. This, of course, gives you a high, super light soufflé. But about halfway through our adolescence, good old Mom went back to show business and her interest in "gourmet cooking" went out the window. We now call her the Queen of Defrost so separating egg whites and beating them into peaks also went out the window.

She blended the beaten eggs (with a spoon) into the cheese-tuna mix. While it may not be as light a dish it tastes just as good, so if you don't feel like separating the eggs, don't bother.

Grease a 1–1/2 quart soufflé or straight-sided casserole dish. Pour in the mixture and bake at 350° for about 45 minutes or until a knife inserted in the center comes out clean. Serve immediately.

Serves 4.

NOTE: You can add an extra can of tuna if you need a more filling dish. It tastes as good, just isn't soufflé light.

CHICKEN

Kiwi Curry Chicken Salad

There is nothing bland about this recipe I picked up in New Zealand. Fortunately kiwi can now be found almost everywhere.

**Chicken breasts (5 if small) skinned,
    or 2 1/4 pounds boned turkey breast
2 1/4 cups dairy sour cream
3/4 cup chutney, finely chopped
1–1 1/2 teaspoons curry powder
1/3 cup toasted shredded coconut
Lettuce
1 orange, peeled and thinly sliced
3 large kiwi, peeled and sliced
1 papaya, peeled and sliced
Chopped fresh mint (optional)**

Place chicken or turkey on steamer rack over 1 cup boiling water. Cover and steam 15 minutes or until thoroughly cooked. Shred meat (should make about 4 cups). Combine sour cream, chutney, curry powder and mix. Add chicken and coconut and mix well. Chill.

Line salad bowl with lettuce and place shredded lettuce in center, then top with chicken mixture.

Garnish

Arrange oranges, kiwi and papaya in circular fashion on top, then sprinkle with chopped mint if used.

Serves 4–6.

Chicken Chili Surprise

6 skinless chicken breasts or thighs, cubed
6 tablespoons cooking oil
4–5 cloves minced garlic
2 sweet red peppers, diced
2–3 jalapeno peppers, seeded and diced
3 tablespoons chili powder
1 tablespoon ground cinnamon
1 teaspoon ground cumin
1 teaspoon ground coriander
1 can (15 ounce) tomato purée
1 can (6 ounce) pitted black olives, sliced
1 cup beer (or chicken broth)
1/4 cup grated unsweetened chocolate

Place 3 tablespoons of oil in large frying pan or Dutch oven and heat on medium high. Sauté onion and garlic for 2–3 minutes, stirring frequently. Add peppers and continue to sauté for 10 minutes, stirring occasionally. Add chili powder, cumin, coriander and cinnamon. Reduce heat and stir. The vegetables can simmer while you heat remaining cooking oil in a 12" fry pan. Add chicken and cook quickly until fork tender. Use a slotted spoon to transfer to vegetable pan. Add olives, beer and tomato puree. Stir.

Add the chocolate and mix well. Simmer on low heat for 15–20 minutes, stirring occasionally. Top with garnishes and serve.

Garnish
Sour cream, chopped avocado, grated cheddar or Monterey Jack cheese.

Serves 6.

Lemon-Mustard Chicken

4 whole chicken breasts, skinned and boned

For Marinade:

1/2 cup lemon juice
1/4 cup Dijon mustard
2 tablespoons fresh basil, chopped
1 tablespoon oregano, chopped
1 tablespoon parsley, chopped
3/4 teaspoon salt (optional)
1/4 teaspoon black pepper

Combine marinade ingredients in bowl and mix well. Place chicken in a large shallow pan. Cover with marinade. Marinate in refrigerator for 3–4 hours. Broil at medium-high until tender or grill on the barbecue for about 6–8 minutes on each side.

Serves 4.

Honey/Orange Chicken

4 chicken breasts
1/2 cup orange juice
1/2 cup honey
1 tablespoon teriyaki
1 teaspoon dry mustard
2 teaspoons cornstarch
1/2 orange thinly sliced

Skin and bone chicken if desired. Mix the cornstarch with a little water to make a smooth paste. Combine this with the remaining ingredients, except for the orange. Marinate the chicken in this mixture for at least 1 hour. Bake at 350° for approximately 1 hour.

Garnish with orange slices, mint leaves.

Serves 4.

Chinese Chicken with Peanuts

2 whole chicken breasts, split, skinned and boned
   or equivalent amount of dark meat
1 tablespoon soy sauce
1 tablespoon white wine, sake or dry sherry
6 green onions, sliced
1/2 teaspoon ground ginger or
1 teaspoon fresh ginger, peeled and minced
1/2 cup orange juice
2 1/2 teaspoons cornstarch
1/4 cup peanut or sesame oil
3/4 cup fresh snow peas
1 red or yellow pepper, sliced into strips
1/2 cup peanuts, preferably chopped coarsely
1/8 teaspoon red pepper flakes (optional)

Cut chicken into bite size pieces. Mix soy sauce, wine, green onions and ginger. Add chicken, toss to coat chicken and set aside to marinate. Mix cornstarch and orange juice and set aside. Heat the oil in a wok or large skillet. Stir-fry the chicken with marinade for about 2 minutes or until chicken is white and tender. Add pea pods, red pepper flakes, peanuts and red pepper. Stir-fry 2 minutes. Stir the orange juice mixture and add to the chicken, stir-fry until slightly thickened. Serve with steamed rice.

Serves 4.

Chicken Stir-Fry

2 cups cooked chicken, chopped
1 1/2 cup broccoli florets
1 red pepper, sliced
2 carrots, julienned

Stir -fry vegetables in oil for about 2 minutes. Add chicken and sauce from above. Cook, stirring constantly, until heated through and sauce thickens. Serve over rice.

Serves 6.

Sauce for Stir-Fry

This a good sauce for chicken stir-fry, but can be used with fish, beef or vegetables.

1/2 cup corn starch
1/4 cup brown sugar, firmly packed
2 teaspoons ginger root, minced
1 large clove garlic, minced
1/2 cup soy sauce
1/4 cup cider vinegar
2 cups chicken or beef broth, cooled
1/2 cup dry sherry or white wine (optional—if you don't use this, add more water)
1/3 cup water

Mix the first 4 ingredients in a 1 quart jar. Add soy sauce and vinegar, shake to mix. Add remaining ingredients and shake well. Store in refrigerator for up to 2 weeks. Shake well before using.

If you like spicy stir-fry, add 1/4 teaspoon red pepper flakes to mixture.

Creamy Turkey and Noodle Bake

6 ounces wide noodles
1 1/2 cups chopped onions
2 cups chopped celery
2 tablespoons butter or margarine
4 cups cooked turkey
10 ounce can cream of mushroom soup
10 ounce can sliced mushrooms, drained

Cook pasta and drain. Sauté onion and celery in butter and add noodles. Add the turkey, mushrooms, and soup. Add salt and pepper to taste. Mix well and place in a large casserole. Bake uncovered at 350° for 35 minutes.

Serves 6.

Chicken with Sour Cream and Mushrooms

1 cut-up fryer or all white or dark pieces, if you prefer
1 can (10 3/4 ounce) cream of mushroom soup
1 small can of mushroom stems and pieces, with liquid
8 ounces sour cream
Onion salt to taste
1/4 cup white wine, dry sherry or water
Paprika

Skin chicken and place in foil lined or greased baking dish.

Combine all ingredients and mix until blended. Pour over chicken, sprinkle generously with paprika. Bake at 350° for 1 hour.

Serves 4.

Lanai Chicken

The ingredients in this dish sound more Italian than Hawaiian but the first time we ate it was on the lanai (balcony) of a gorgeous penthouse overlooking the ocean and crescent-shaped beach of Waikiki.

This dish is simple to assemble and can be done early in the day. If you are holding it to bake later, don't add the sauce until you are ready to put it in the oven. This may be cooked individually or arranged in a baking dish for multiple servings.

4 large chicken breasts
4 slices mozzarella cheese
4 canned chiles
Seasoned bread crumbs, such as Prego
Tomato sauce

Remove skin from chicken breasts, wash and pat dry. With a sharp knife, slice through center to make a pocket.

Stuff pocket with a slice of cheese. Flatten and lay chile on top of cheese. Pinch pocket closed. If you wish, you can close opening with a tooth pick or skewer, but it is not a necessity. (If some cheese seeps out during cooking, just spoon under chicken before serving.)

Brush chicken with tomato sauce, roll in crumbs until heavily coated. Arrange in greased baking dish.

When ready to bake, cover with thin layer of tomato sauce.

If you are a tomato sauce lover, make extra to be spooned over chicken before serving.

Bake in 350° oven for approximately 30 minutes or until chicken is done and crumbs lightly browned.

Serves 4.

MOA HA'ARI / Tahitian Chicken

This is a cooked chicken, mixed in a cream sauce made with coconut milk and heated thoroughly. For a touch of French Polynesia, serve it in a hollowed out half of a coconut shell. Pipe mashed potatoes around the edge. Glaze the center with hollandaise sauce. Then pop it under the broiler for a minute or so. I have made it in a casserole but it's fun to find something different for a serving place that adds the Polynesian touch.

3/4–1 cup cooked white meat of chicken per person
1 cup white sauce per person, add more if too thick
Hollandaise sauce—packaged mix does work well with this dish

Sauce:

1 ounce butter or margarine
1 cup all purpose flour
1/3 cup cornstarch
1 quart coconut milk (canned or frozen)
1 1/2 quarts milk
1/2 ounce chicken base (boullion cubes will work)
Dash of salt and white pepper

Makes about 10–12 cups.

Cook and blend over low heat as you would any cream sauce. DO NOT USE ALL OF FLOUR at beginning. Start with half, then add, if necessary, for thickness you desire. When thoroughly heated and smooth, add heated chicken. Spoon into a baking container.

Glaze top of cream mixture with the hollandaise sauce. Place under broiler for a minute or two to heat.

Garnish with piped hot mashed potatoes around the serving piece rim. Dust with a dash of paprika.

A nice tropical touch is to place a vanda orchid on the dish. Also adding Ti leaves or lemon leaves as a doily under the server. Almost all florists carry lemon leaves and many now have Ti leaves available.

Chicken with Green and White Noodles

1/4 pound white noodles
1/4 pound spinach noodles
6 tablespoons butter or margarine
6 tablespoons flour
2 cups chicken broth
1/4 cup sherry
1/2 cup heavy cream
1/2 pound fresh mushrooms, diced
2 1/2 cups cooked chicken, shredded
Salt and pepper to taste
Grated Parmesan cheese

Cook noodles until firm, drain and put in greased casserole.

Sauce

Melt butter, slowly add flour, mix until it forms a ball. Add broth a little at a time, using wire whisk to blend in liquid until smooth and a thick paste is formed. Blend in salt, pepper and sherry, stir and add in cream a little at a time. Remove from stove, add mushrooms and chicken. Gently fold into noodles. Sprinkle top of mixture with Parmesan cheese and dot with butter or margarine. Bake in preheated oven, 350° for 20–30 minutes or until top is brown and sauce bubbling.

Serves 4.

Honey Chicken

1 cut-up fryer
1 egg, beaten
1 cup honey
2 tablespoons lemon juice
1/4 cup soy sauce
1 1/2 teaspoons paprika

Skin chicken and place in foil lined or greased baking dish. Combine all ingredients, whisk very briskly to blend well. Pour over chicken and marinate for several hours, turning chicken occasionally. Bake at 325° for 1 hour 15 minutes, turning chicken several times.

Serves 4.

Mustard Chicken

Do not be put off by the amount of mustard in the ingredient list. The first time I made it, I held my breath wondering if the mustard flavor would be overpowering. It is not and many people don't even realize it has a mustard sauce base.

1 cut-up fryer
1/2 cup prepared mustard
1/2 cup Dijon mustard
1/2 cup soy sauce
1/2 cup Worcestershire sauce
1/2 cup lemon juice
1/4 cup vegetable or olive oil
1/4 cup brown sugar, packed
1/2 teaspoon garlic powder
Salt and pepper to taste

Skin chicken and place in foil lined or greased baking dish. Combine all ingredients and mix until blended. Pour over chicken and marinate for at least 3 hours, or preferably overnight, turning occasionally. Bake at 325° for 1 hour 15 minutes, basting occasionally.

HINT: This marinade also works well for baking whole chickens or Cornish game hens.

MEAT

Beef, Beef and More Beef

If you'll try to keep an open mind about leftovers, you'll not only save cooking time, but money as well. Let's start with a roast. Buy one at least 2 to 4 pounds larger than what you need for a meal. Season with a good mixture of seasoning salt such as Lawrys, Beau Monde or Schimmel Seasoning and roast as usual. Make it as rare as possible for your taste. That will help it keep from being too dry for the other dishes.

As soon as possible before serving, cut enough slices for sandwiches, then dice the remaining extra meat into cubes and save for stew or stroganoff. Refrigerate or freeze immediately depending on when you plan on using it.

Build your own Sandwich Board

Slices from this beef, as well as turkey, ham and chicken can be stockpiled until you have enough to use. Arrange meat across one half of a serving board. Line assorted flavors of bread below it. Then add dishes of mustard, ketchup, mayonnaise and any other desired dressing. Garnishes of lettuce, sliced tomatoes, onions, olives add color as well as texture. This makes a good lunch. Add a thick soup and you have a light supper.

Ann Lander's Famous Meat Loaf

Ann Landers is a "shirttail" relative and was kind enough to give me permission to use her recipe. She has printed it numerous times in her column but if you have not used it before you are in for a treat. When I made it on the boat I always had to make sure there would be enough left over for cold meat loaf sandwiches the next day because everyone loved it.

    2 pounds ground round steak
    2 eggs
    1–1/2 cup bread crumbs
    3/4 cup ketchup
    1 teaspoon Accent
    1/2 cup warm water
    1 package Lipton's onion soup mix
    1 can (8 ounce) tomato sauce

Combine all ingredients except the tomato sauce and mix thoroughly. Put into a loaf pan; cover with 2 strips of bacon if you like that flavor. Pour the tomato sauce over all. Bake at 350° for 1 hour.

Serves 4–6.

Don's Delite

My friend Don can cook as well as a Cordon Blu graduate but being a Hollywood set decorator leaves him little time for his hobby unless he's "between engagements" as they say. The fact that he may have to be on the set at 6 a.m. and put in a ten to twelve hour day does not stop him from entertaining, even if it is just a simple meal. This dish may be made ahead and reheated at the last minute.

1 pound hamburger
1/2 cup chopped onion (optional)
1/2 teaspoon seasoning salt such as Lawrys, Beau Monde, etc.
2 cups green beans, cooked firm as they may continue cooking during baking period. If using frozen beans, do not cook.
1 can (10 3/4 ounce) condensed tomato soup
5 medium size cooked potatoes
OR 4 servings of packaged instant mashed potatoes
1/2 cup warm milk
1 beaten egg
1/2 cup shredded American cheese (optional)

If you have a large casserole that can be used for stovetop cooking, this can be prepared and served in one pot. If not, in a large skillet cook the meat and onion until meat is lightly browned. Drain off excess fat, if any. Add seasoning salt and pepper. Stir in cooked beans and soup; pour into greased casserole, 1 1/2 to 2 quart size.

Spoon mashed potato mounds around edge of casserole. If using cooked potatoes, mash while hot; add milk and egg. If using instant packaged potatoes, prepare according to directions, except add milk a little at a time so that mixture remains stiff enough to hold its shape. Sprinkle potatoes with cheese and bake at 350° for 25 to 30 minutes.

Serves 4–6.

Calzone

2 loaves frozen white bread dough
10 ounce carton frozen broccoli/cauliflower
combination, thawed
1 pound hamburger, cooked
1 onion, sliced or chopped
1 green or red pepper, chopped
16 ounces mozzarella cheese, shredded

Let bread dough rise, according to package instructions.

Roll each loaf out into a rectangle about 1/2 inch thick. Layer each loaf with a combination of the ingredients. Cover with the cheese. Bring the sides of the dough together and pinch shut. Wetting your fingers helps seal the dough. Fold ends up and seal shut. Place on a greased cookie sheet and let rise for about 45 minutes. Bake at 350° for 25 minutes.

Serves 6–8.

HINT: Great to serve in slices for parties.

Fluffy Hamburger

If you like a moist, lighter hamburger or meat loaf you'll find this the base for several variations.

1/4–1/2 cup tomato juice
1/2 cup uncooked instant or fast cook oatmeal

Cheeseburger Loaf

2 pounds hamburger
1/4–1/2 cup tomato juice
1/2 tablespoon seasoning salt
1/2 cup uncooked instant or fast cook oatmeal
4–5 slices of cheese, white or yellow according to preference

Moisten oatmeal in juice, then mix all together.

Pat half of meat mix in a loaf pan, then lay strips of cheese along top. Add rest of meat mixture, then criss-cross remaining cheese strips along the top. You can "frost" top with a few spoonfuls of ketchup or barbecue sauce. Any type of cheese that melts will work but DO NOT use something like Velveeta as it melts too much and will run down to the bottom of the pan rather than stay in place.

Bake 350° for 50 minutes.

Serves 4–5.

Hamburger or Ground Turkey Bake

8 slices white bread
1 tablespoon margarine
1/2 pound hamburger or ground turkey
2 tablespoons celery, chopped
1/4 cup onion, chopped
1 tablespoon mustard, prepared or Dijon
1 cup cheddar or jack cheese, shredded
2 eggs, slightly beaten
1 cup milk
Onion salt and pepper to taste

Remove crust from bread. Spread 4 slices of bread lightly with margarine. Arrange in an 8" x 8" pan square baking dish. Toast both sides lightly, in a 350° oven. Brown meat, onions and celery.

Drain fat off and mix in the mustard. Spread over the bread. Cover with the cheese. Place remaining bread over the cheese. Combine the eggs, milk, and any seasonings and mix well. Pour this mixture over the bread. Let soak for 20–30 minutes. Bake at 350° for 45 minutes.

Serves 4.

Hamburger Stroganoff

12 ounce package of spinach noodles, cooked according to
   package
1/2 cup onion, minced
1 clove garlic, minced OR 1 teaspoon garlic salt
1/4 cup margarine
1 pound hamburger
2 tablespoons flour
Salt and pepper to taste
8 ounce can sliced mushrooms or 1 pound fresh mushrooms
10 ounce can cream of chicken soup
1 cup sour cream
Paprika

Sauté onion and garlic in margarine. Add hamburger and brown. Drain grease if necessary, add flour, salt, pepper, and mushrooms, cook about 5 minutes. Add soup and simmer uncovered for 10 minutes. Stir in sour cream. Heat through. Serve on top of noodles. Sprinkle generously with paprika.

Serves 4.

Red Hawaiian Meatballs

I was given this recipe in Hawaii. It is a bit on the sweet side but can be a main course as well as an appetizer. I've made them early in the day and left them on low in a crock pot for several hours. You could freeze the meatballs, then defrost and add sauce, let warm thoroughly on low heat so that the flavor of the sauce permeates. I have never frozen the sauce but you could experiment with it since they do freeze cranberry sauce in commercial dinners.

2 pounds ground beef (or even ground turkey but if you use turkey do not heat until ready to serve as turkey can spoil easily)
1 cup cracker crumbs, finely ground
1/4 cup dried parsley
1/3 cup ketchup
1 tablespoon brown sugar
2 eggs
2 tablespoons Worcestershire sauce

Mix well and form into balls. Makes about 25 small cocktail size. If you want to use for a main dish, make them larger.

Can be browned on a cookie sheet for about 20 minutes, medium oven or sauted in Teflon fry pan. Drain well.

Sauce

1 pound can clear cranberry sauce
1 tablespoon lemon juice
12 ounce bottle chili sauce
2 tablespoons brown sugar

Heat all ingredients until dissolved. Place meat balls in a 10" x 15" pan. Pour sauce over and bake uncovered 350° degrees for about 35 minutes. Baste during baking time.

HINT: For an extra island touch, add 1/2 cup canned diced pineapple to sauce.

Maui Meat Loaf

This year I'm living in Kula, Maui. Our house is situated half way up Haleakala, one of Hawaii's most beautiful, inactive volcanoes.

2 pounds lean ground beef
1 egg, beaten
1 cup chopped Maui onions
1/2 cup bread crumbs
1/2 cup barbecue sauce
2 tablespoons chopped parsley
1/2 cup finely chopped Hawaiian Macadamia nuts

Bake for one hour in a 300° oven.

Serves 8.

NOTE: There are a variety of "flavored" barbecue sauces. We get a Kiawe wood one in the islands that has a very distinctive flavor and is sometimes available in other areas. It is the island version of mesquite which is found in many prepared sauces.

This recipe features Maui onions. Maui onions are sweeter and not as strong flavored as regular onions. Get a friend to bring some back or they can be shipped from specialty stores.

Cajun Meat Loaf

1/2 cup green onions, chopped
1 cup red, green and yellow peppers, diced
1 1/2 cup onion, diced
1/3 cup celery, diced
1 1/4 tablespoons Worcestershire sauce
2 tablespoons Cajun spices, or to taste
1/3 cup milk
1 pound lean ground beef
3/4 pound ground pork (may use only ground beef if you prefer)
2 eggs
1-2 small jalapeno chilies, depending on how hot you want it
1/4 cup unsalted butter
1/4-1/2 teaspoon cayenne pepper
1 tablespoon hot pepper sauce
2 bay leaves
1/3 cup Heinz 57 Sauce
1/3 cup ketchup
3/4 cup bread crumbs

Sauté onions, peppers, celery and jalapenos in butter until tender (about 10 minutes).

Add cayenne, hot pepper sauce, Worcestershire sauce, bay leaves, and Cajun spices. Sauté for 5 minutes.

Add milk, Heinz 57 Sauce and ketchup. Simmer for 5 minutes.

Remove from heat and add meat, eggs and crumbs. Mix well.

Pack into a 9" x 5" loaf pan, preferably glass. Cover with foil. Bake in a pan of hot water at 350° for 30 minutes. Remove the foil and bake another 30 minutes. Cool before slicing.

Serves 8.

Peppered Beef Brisket

4 pounds brisket
1/4 cup cracked black pepper
1 teaspoon ground cardamom

Combine cardamom and pepper and pound into meat, using the heel of your hand.

Marinade for Peppered Beef

2/3 cup soy sauce
1/2 cup vinegar, white or cider
1 tablespoon ketchup
1 teaspoon paprika
1 clove of garlic, minced

Combine all ingredients, pour over meat, marinate overnight.

Cover with foil and bake at 300° for 3–3 1/2 hours.

Serves 6–8.

HINT: Even lean brisket shrinks when cooked at the lowest temperature so allow for that when buying the meat. Allow to cool before attempting to slice it. If you have the time, make the day before, slice and re-heat. This is one dish that is literally as good, or better, re-heated. Freezes very well.

Mystery Sauce Brisket

4 pounds beef brisket
1/2 cup ketchup
1/2 cup chili sauce
1/4 cup Worcestershire sauce
1/8 cup lemon juice
1/8 cup Heinz 57 sauce
1/4 cup hickory smoked barbecue sauce
1/4 cup grape jelly
Tenderizing salt

This is another recipe that is very popular with the film crews. It makes an exotic barbecue beef dish that works very well in sandwich form as well as sliced like roast beef.

Sprinkle meat with tenderizer and let sit at least one hour.

Mix other ingredients, pour over meat and marinate overnight, if possible. Cook 4–5 hours at 275°.

Serves 6.

Beef Stew

1 pound stew meat
10 ounce carton, frozen green beans
10 ounce carton, frozen corn OR 1 15 ounce can corn
1 small can artichokes, drained and halved
1 small can black olives, pitted and drained
10–12 small new or red potatoes
3 carrots, cut into bite-size pieces
2 cups broccoli florets
1 onion, chopped
1 can (15 ounce) stewed tomatoes
1/2–1 can beer
1 can (15 ounce) tomato juice
1 tablespoon basil, chopped
2 teaspoons tarragon
Onion and garlic powder, salt and pepper to taste

In large skillet, brown meat.

Combine all ingredients in a large pot and simmer for at least 2–3 hours.

Serves 4–6.

HINT: The longer this stew simmers, the better the flavors mix. If you have the time, 4–5 hours simmering time is great. I have simmered this on low heat all night, allowed dish to cool and frozen it before going out on the boats. Simply thaw and reheat when needed.

Turkish Stuffed Peppers and Tomatoes

Stuffed peppers have been around for a long time, but this dish adds a bit of color and introduces a contrasting flavor.

Because fat content in hamburger varies, it is difficult to suggest an exact amount. For this recipe, it is simpler to list filling for one pepper or tomato and let you multiply for the number you will be using.

1/2–3/4 cup cooked hamburger or minced lamb
4 tablespoons cooked rice
1/8 teaspoon fresh chopped parsley
1–2 tablespoons chopped onion
1/8 teaspoon dried mint
4–6 ounces tomato juice

Slice the tops off the peppers and tomatoes. Save tops. Scoop out seeds and pith. Turn tomatoes upside down to drain.

Make stuffing of meat, rice, parsley, onion and mint. If meat is very lean, you can add 1 tablespoon of margarine to mix.

Stuff peppers and tomatoes with mixture.

Place side by side in a baking dish. Pour half of tomato juice in center of each pepper and tomato. Replace the tops. Pour remaining tomato juice and about a half cup water into bottom of baking dish.

Bake for 30 minutes at 325°.

HINT: Because the tomato is a softer texture and could finish cooking sooner, get extra firm ones.

Colorful variation: In same baking dish, add one or two red peppers, stuffed with rice only. Cook rice, using package directions for the more moist version. Drain, stuff and cook with other vegetables. To prevent rice from drying out, cover with foil, or place in oven about 10 minutes after you have started baking the other ones.

VEGETABLES AND SIDE DISHES

Couscous

As stuffing for fowl or as side dish, couscous is a Middle East pasta that is fairly bland but may be mixed with broth and seasonings for an unusual flavored starch. Most supermarkets stock this item so it is no longer necessary to hunt out a specialty grocery store.

Couscous, cooked according to package directions.

Add: slivered almonds, chopped onion, diced, peeled apple and raisins. All items are traditional but you may skip any that do not appeal to your personal taste without doing an injustice to the flavor.

Make chicken broth. Add curry powder to taste and mix into couscous.

If you prefer a milder taste, just use beef or chicken broth.

Kasha (Buckwheat Kernels)

Kasha is another interesting starch to replace rice. Like couscous, it works well with a variety of added ingredients.

Stir one well beaten egg into one cup uncooked kasha. Dampen your palms with water, then rub mixture between your palms until kernels tend to separate. This will bring out the nutty flavor of the buckwheat and also helps to keep it from getting mushy.

Put mixture into two quart pan or skillet, and heat for a minute or two in order to set egg and separate kernels. Push mix to side of pan, add 2 tablespoons butter, margarine or scant 1/4 cup of oil. You can then lightly sauté 1/2 cup chopped onion, celery or mushrooms, adding salt and pepper to taste.

Now add 2 cups boiling liquid—can be water but chicken or beef broth or consommé gives it more flavor. Cover pan tightly and cook gently over low heat for 10 to 15 minutes until kasha grains are tender.

It is now ready to serve. My favorite version is to add about 8 ounces of hot, cooked bowknot noodles at this point.

This recipe makes about 3 cups.

Black Bean Salad

This may be served as a side dish, or by adding leftover meat or fish, it could be used for a light lunch.

1 can drained black beans
1 package (10 ounce) frozen corn, cooked
1 green pepper, chopped
1 red pepper, chopped
1 Jalapeno pepper, seeded and chopped
3 green onions, thinly sliced
2 tablespoons minced parsley
2 tablespoons virgin olive oil
3 tablespoons lime juice

Combine all ingredients. Chill for at least 2 hours. Serve in hollowed out, drained tomato, or on a bed of lettuce.

Warm Green Bean Salad

1–1/2 pounds fresh green beans, ends cut off
1/4 cup green onions, chopped
1 red pepper, sliced
1 teaspoon Dijon mustard
1/4 cup balsamic vinegar
3/4 cup extra light olive oil
Salt and pepper to taste
1/2 teaspoon dill or basil (optional)

Steam green beans for 4–5 minutes or until tender but crisp. Drain. Combine green onions, mustard, vinegar and olive oil in a small bowl and mix well. Season to taste with salt, pepper and herbs.

Place the warm beans in a large bowl. Add the red peppers and toss with enough of the dressing to coat the vegetables.

Spinach Rice

2 ounces butter or margarine
2 cloves garlic, optional
1 1/2 cups long grain rice
2 1/2 cups water
6 stalks spinach
Salt and pepper to taste

Heat butter or margarine in pan. Add crushed garlic and rice, stir to coat rice with butter. Add the water, salt and pepper.

Bring to a boil, reduce heat, gently simmer uncovered until liquid has almost been absorbed (about 10 minutes). Stir occasionally.

Wash spinach thoroughly to get rid of sandy dirt. Chop leaves in fine pieces and stir into rice. Continue cooking on lowest heat for about 5 more minutes.

Persian Rice

White rice, enough for 6 servings
1 large onion, thinly sliced
1/2 cup carrots, grated
2 tablespoons orange peel, grated
1/3 cup raisins
1/3 cup slivered almonds OR
1/3 cup pine nuts

Cook rice according to directions on the package.

Sauté remaining ingredients in 1/4 cup of butter or margarine. Add to cooked rice and toss gently.

Green Noodles

My mother fell in love with a baked green noodle casserole that was featured in a Rush Street restaurant in Chicago. We've experimented with several white sauces and while none seems to be quite the same dish, we think this version holds up well. Because we prefer white cheeses, we have never experimented with a yellow cheese-based sauce but it might make a good substitute.

> **1 large package spinach noodles, cooked according to package directions. (Undercook as it will be baking in a sauce.)**
> **1 1/2–2 cups thick white sauce, preferably made with half and half instead of milk.**
> **1 cup shredded Swiss cheese. (Mix half in the white sauce.)**

Mix together and put in greased baking dish. Sprinkle remaining Swiss cheese evenly over top, then dust this with Parmesan cheese. Bake 325° until cheese melts. You may pop it under the broiler for a minute to form a brown crust.

Serves 8–10.

Low-Cal Cheese Dressed Onion Pasta

This flavorful dish only has 292 calories but is quite filling.

> **4 cups cooked, small shell macaroni.**
> **2 medium red or yellow onions—thin slice lengthwise**
> **3 tablespoon olive oil**
> **2–3 cloves minced garlic**
> **2 cups chicory, lettuce or spinach, torn into bite-size pieces**
> **1/4 cup grated Romano or Parmesan cheese**
> **1 tablespoon chopped fresh basil**
> **Ground pepper, if desired**

Over medium heat, sauté onion in two tablespoons of the olive oil. Cook about five minutes until translucent. Stir in garlic, then remove from burner and cool. In large serving bowl, toss onion-garlic mix with remaining spoon of olive oil and other ingredients. Chill thoroughly before serving.

Serves 4.

Linguine with Herbed Avocado Cream Sauce

3 avocadoes, peeled and pitted
3/4 cup water
3 teaspoons fresh lemon juice
1 1/2 teaspoons of each of the following (dried and crumbled): parsley, basil, tarragon
3/4 teaspoon of each of following (dried and crumbled): tarragon, dillweed, thyme
Salt and pepper
3 tablespoons butter or margarine
1 1/2 cups whipping cream
1 1/2 pounds freshly cooked linguine

Purée first eleven ingredients in blender or processor. Melt butter in heavy sauce pan over medium to low heat. Add avocado mixture and heat through, stirring occasionally. Stir in cream. Cook until thickened, about three minutes. Pour over pasta and serve immediately.

Serves 8-10.

Baked Noodle Ring

1 package broad noodles
4 eggs
1 cup cream
2 tablespoons Worcestershire sauce
1/2 cup ketchup
1/2 cup grated American cheese (optional)
Salt and Paprika

Cook noodles in boiling, salted water for ten minutes. Drain and rinse in cold water. Beat eggs until light, add remaining ingredients and mix with noodles. Pour into a buttered and floured ring mold and place in a pan of boiling water. Cover with a lid or foil and bake at 350° for thirty minutes, until firm. You can fill the center with vegetables.

Serves 6-8.

Bubi's Baked Noodles

If you like noodles with a lot of cheese, this dish is for you. My great-grandmother used to make this and I'll put her noodles up against anyone's for it's creamy texture.

- **1 pound package noodles, cooked according to package and drained**
- **10 ounce carton cottage cheese**
- **1 scant cup sour cream**
- **5 eggs**
- **1 stick butter, melted.**

Blend cottage cheese, sour cream, eggs and butter. Stir into noodles. Pour into greased pan. Bake at 350° until brown on top, about 1 1/2 hours but watch during last half hour as oven temperatures vary and you don't want it to get dried out.

You can offer a side dish of extra sour cream. Some simple but tasty variations are:

Brown bread crumbs in butter and a bit of seasoning salt and sprinkle over boiled noodles.

Sprinkle buttered noodles with caraway seed or dillweed.

Serves 6–8.

Mama Ruth's Barley/Mushroom Casserole

This is one of my Grandmother Ruth's recipes. You'll get lots of rave reviews with this one.

3 tablespoons butter or margarine
1 beef boullion cube, dissolved in 3/4 cup water
2 cans onion soup
1 1/2 cup barley
6 ounces can mushroom stems and pieces, with liquid

Melt butter or margarine in a large skillet or electric fry pan. Add barley and brown. Add remaining ingredients. Bring to a boil over medium-high heat. Stir well and pour into a greased 2 quart casserole. Cover and bake at 350° for 1 hour. Check after 30 minutes; if all liquid has absorbed you can add another 1/2–3/4 cup of water and stir into casserole.

Serves 6.

Marinated Mushrooms

1 pound fresh mushrooms, if large cut in half
1 medium green pepper, sliced
1 medium red pepper, sliced
1 onion, sliced
1/2 cup butter or margarine

Sauce

2 tablespoons Dijon mustard
2 tablespoons Worcestershire sauce
1/2 cup brown sugar
3/4 cup red wine
1 teaspoon basil
Salt and pepper to taste

Sauté onion, mushrooms and peppers in butter for 5 minutes. Mix everything for the sauce, except the wine, into a smooth paste. Add the wine and blend well. Add to the mushroom mixture and simmer for 45 minutes.

Serves 6.

Zucchini Casserole

Because of the eggs and cheese. This dish could serve as a light lunch alternative.

2 tablespoons butter or margarine
6 medium zucchini, cut in 1/4 inch slices
1 1/2 teaspoon Italian seasoning, optional
1/2 teaspoon salt
1/4 teaspoon pepper
1/4 teaspoon garlic powder
5 eggs
1 cup (4 ounces shredded) Provolone cheese
1 1/4 cup half and half
2 tablespoons flour
1 tablespoon grated Romano cheese

Melt butter in large skillet. Sauté zucchini and seasonings until crisp-tender, about five minutes. Set aside.

Beat eggs until foamy. Stir in cream, Provolone cheese and flour. Add zucchini and pour into buttered 1 1/2 quart baking dish. Sprinkle Romano cheese over top.

Bake at 325° until knife inserted near center comes out clean, about 40 minutes. Let stand five minutes before serving.

Serves 6–8.

Stuffed Zucchini

2 pounds small zucchini
2 eggs, slightly beaten
1/3 cup fine bread crumbs
1/3 cup Parmesan or Romano cheese, grated
1/4 cup vegetable oil
1 onion, minced
1 tablespoon parsley, minced
Garlic salt to taste
Tarragon to taste

Wash zucchini and cut off ends.

Parboil whole zucchini in boiling water for 15 minutes. Drain and cool slightly. Cut lengthwise in halves. Carefully scoop out pulp with a spoon, leaving a shell. Mash the pulp and mix with the remaining ingredients.

Place the shells in a greased 13" x 9" pan. Fill the shells with the pulp mixture. Bake at 350° for 30 minutes.

Serves 4.

Spaghetti Squash Mexicana

1 3–4 pound spaghetti squash, cooked
8 ounces jalapeno cheese, shredded
1/2 cup corn or nacho tortilla chips, crushed
1 can (16 ounce) stewed tomatoes
Parmesan cheese, grated

After cooking and shredding the spaghetti squash, put half of it in the bottom of a greased 10" x 6" baking dish. Sprinkle with half of the cheese and chips. Layer the remaining squash, cheese and chips.

Pour stewed tomatoes over the top and bake at 350° for about 20 minutes or until heated thoroughly. Sprinkle with Parmesan cheese and bake 5 more minutes.

If the jalapeno cheese is too spicy you may use cheddar or half jalapeno and half cheddar or Jack cheese.

Squash and Stuff

1 large yellow summer squash, unpeeled and cut into thin strips
1 large zucchini, peeled and cut into thin strips
1 small green bell pepper, cut into thin strips
1 small sweet red pepper, cut into thin strips
1/2 teaspoon dried oregano
1 1/2 tablespoons olive oil
Salt and pepper to taste

Heat oil in frying pan over medium heat. Add onion and sauté for 5 minutes. Add squash, zucchini and peppers. Stir-fry until the vegetables are tender but crisp—about 5–6 minutes. Mix in seasonings and serve immediately.

Garnish

After heating, add Greek olives and crumbled Feta cheese for a Greek flavor.

Serves 4.

HINT: When cooking with olive oil, never get the oil too hot. That is the reason many Greek dishes are served lukewarm.

Acorn Squash Rings

2 acorn squash
1/3 stick margarine or butter, melted
Brown sugar, or date sugar

Preheat oven to 350°.

Cut squash into half inch thick rings. Clean out fiber and seeds from center of the rings. Place rings on a greased cookie sheet. Brush each ring with melted margarine. Sprinkle with brown sugar or date sugar which is not quite as sweet. Bake until tender, about 20–25 minutes.

Serves 4.

A colorful two vegetable dish can be made by adding cooked peas to the center of the rings.

Ginger Carrots

3–5 medium-sized carrots
1/2 cup chicken broth (or water with chicken bullion cube)
1 teaspoon grated ginger root or 1/4 teaspoon powdered ginger
1 teaspoon sugar
2 tablespoons margarine

You lose a lot of the vitamin content when you peel carrots, so unless the slight darkening really bothers you, don't peel them.

Slice in strips, simmer in broth over low heat for about ten minutes or until tender.

Add ginger, sugar and margarine. Cook for 2–3 minutes, turning carrots carefully to coat them.

Garnish with minced parsley. I have a friend who adds a few golden raisins when she makes this dish giving it a sweeter taste.

Serves 4.

Honey and Cinnamon Glazed Carrots

1 pound carrots
1/2 cup water
1 tablespoon margarine
1/4 teaspoon cinnamon
1 tablespoon honey
1 teaspoon lemon juice

Cut carrots into 3" strips or slices. Put in skillet with water and melted margarine. Cover and steam until crisp-tender—about 5–10 minutes. If water has not evaporated, drain and add rest of ingredients. Simmer until ingredients blend thoroughly.

Serves 4.

Onions and Carrots

1 pound carrots
1 package frozen whole onions (16 ounces)
1/4 cup margarine
2 tablespoons brown sugar
1/4 teaspoon ground ginger
1/4 teaspoon salt

Peel and cut carrots into 1/2 inch slices.

Bring about one inch of water to a boil. Put in carrots, cover, and simmer for about 10 minutes. Add onions. Cover and cook about 5 minutes or until vegetables just tender. Drain and return to pan. Add margarine, brown sugar, ginger and salt. Stir frequently, cooking over medium heat for about 5 minutes or until vegetables are glazed.

NOTE: *If you do not care for the flavor of ginger, you might try using a dash of curry powder instead.*

Serves 4.

Blue whales are the largest creatures to ever have lived on earth, even larger than the dinosaurs. Can be up to 100 feet long and weigh 100 tons.

Broccoli Rice Casserole

1 tablespoon butter or margarine
1 tablespoon vegetable oil
1 clove garlic, minced
1/2 cup onion, chopped fine
1 2/3 cups chicken broth
1 cup water
1/4 teaspoon nutmeg
Salt and pepper to taste
1 cup brown rice
2 cups broccoli florets, cut small
1 cup halved cherry tomatoes

Melt butter and oil in a large sauce pan. Sauté garlic and onion for 2 minutes. Add the broth, water and spices. Bring to a boil and add the rice. When it returns to a boil, reduce heat, cover and simmer for 40 minutes.

Put broccoli on top of rice, cover and simmer about 10 minutes or until all the liquid is absorbed. Stir in the tomatoes. Cover and heat thoroughly.

You can add julienned zucchini or carrots, or sliced mushrooms along with the broccoli.

Serves 8.

Esther's Fabulous Broccoli Casserole

2 packages (10 ounce) of chopped broccoli, thawed
2 cans (10–3/4 ounce) of cream of chicken soup
3 cups white rice, cooked according to directions on package
1 large jar of Cheeze Whiz

Mix all ingredients together and place in a large casserole. Top with buttered bread crumbs and bake at 325° for 30 minutes or until heated through and the top is lightly browned.

Pea Duo with Mint

This may be served cold as a salad dish.

1 1/2 cups shelled fresh peas, or frozen peas
8 ounces snow peas (Chinese peas), trim ends
1 cup fresh mint leaves, chopped
1/4 cup Hellmann's mayonnaise
1/4 cup sour cream
Salt and pepper to taste
1/4 cup crumbled cooked bacon or artificial bacon bits

Mix mayonnaise, sour cream and seasoning, set aside.

Cook peas in boiling water until barely tender, about two minutes. Drain.

In a second pan, cook snow peas until bright green but still crisp, 30–45 seconds. Drain.

Mix two peas together in one pan, gently folding in the chopped mint. Add the cream mixture, blend carefully and heat on low fire just till the sauce is warm.

Serves 4–6.

Garnishes

Sprinkle the bacon over the dish. You can also arrange snow peas like the spokes of a wheel or leave a few sprigs of whole mint leaves and cluster in the center of the bowl.

If you are watching your cholesterol level, there are some artificial sour creams on the market that work very well.

Roasted New Potatoes—Danish Style

20 small red potatoes
1/2 cup (1 stick) butter or margarine
1 teaspoon salt
Dash pepper, optional
1/4 cup finely chopped dill

Scrub and dry potatoes. Melt butter or margarine in pan with tight-fitting lid. Add potatoes, sprinkle with seasoning. Cover pan and roast potatoes over medium high heat, shaking the pan often. Cook for about 12 minutes, or until tender—do not overcook. Add dill and shake pan again to distribute evenly over the potatoes. Allow 3-4 potatoes per serving depending on how small they are.

HINT: Dust bottom of pan with very thin layer of granulated sugar after you have melted the butter. It can give the potatoes a crispier taste.

Zesty Potato Medley

2 1/2 pounds new potatoes, steamed until tender
6 tablespoons olive oil
3 tablespoons wine vinegar
1 tablespoon Dijon mustard
3/4 cup sweet red pepper, diced
1/2 cup celery, diced
1/2 cup sweet peas
1 cup sour cream
1 tablespoon fresh tarragon, chopped
OR 1 1/2 teaspoons dried
Salt and pepper to taste

Cube potatoes. While still warm, toss gently with oil, vinegar, salt and pepper. Blend sour cream, tarragon and mustard. Mix all ingredients together. Chill.

Potato—Vegetable Latkes

Latkes are potato pancakes. By adding vegetables to the batter of grated potato, you get an unusual side dish that will go with almost any meat or fowl entree.

2 medium potatoes, pared and coarsely shredded (2 1/2 cups)
2 large zucchini, unpared and shredded (2 1/2 cups)
1 large carrot, shredded (1 cup)
1/4 chopped onion
3 tablespoons flour
1/4 chopped parsley
1 teaspoon salt
1/2 teaspoon pepper
3 eggs, lightly beaten
3 tablespoons margarine

Squeeze shredded potato and zucchini between paper towels until very dry. In large bowl, combine with carrot, onion, flour, parsley, salt, pepper and eggs. Mix well. Melt margarine in large skillet over medium heat. Drop in heaping tablespoonfuls of potato mix. Flatten slightly. Cook until golden brown, then turn to brown other side. Place cooked pancakes on baking sheet in warm oven, then repeat until all of the mixture is used.

Makes 16 latkes.

Potato Soufflé

8 large potatoes
8 ounces cream cheese, room temperature
8 ounces sour cream
2 teaspoons garlic salt
3 teaspoons chives, chopped fine
4 tablespoons butter or margarine
Paprika

Peel potatoes and boil in large covered pan until tender. Drain and mash well. Using an electric mixer, beat cream cheese and sour cream until well blended. Beat into potatoes until very smooth. Blend in garlic and chives. Turn into buttered shallow 3–4 quart casserole. Dot with butter and sprinkle with paprika.

Bake covered at 400° for 1 hour or until top is lightly browned and crusty.

Serves 12–15 easily.

May be made up to 3 days ahead of time and refrigerated. Bring to room temperature and then bake as directed.

Orcas or killer whales are actually the largest dolphins. They received the title "whale killer" because these whales will occasionally feed on other marine mammals including other whales, sea lions, dolphins or seals. Over the years the term "whale killer" got turned around, and the name stuck.

Maui Macadamia Nut Stuffed Eggplant

This dish has a bit more flavor and texture than most eggplant recipes.

2 medium-sized eggplants
1/2 teaspoon salt
1 teaspoon sugar
1 small onion, chopped
2 tablespoons margarine
2 tablespoons ketchup
1 teaspoon soy sauce
1 large egg, beaten
1/2 cup chopped macadamia nuts
1/3 cup buttered bread crumbs
Dash of pepper

Cut eggplants in half lengthwise, cook in boiling water for 15 minutes, no longer.

Drain. When cooled, scoop out the centers, leaving a shell about 1/4 inch thick. Turn upside down to drain on paper towels.

Chop the pulp and cook in salted water until tender. Drain.

While pulp is cooking, saute onions in margarine. Add onions and seasonings to the cooked pulp, reserve bread crumbs.

Scoop filling into the eggplant shells, then sprinkle the top of each with the crumbs.

Place in greased baking dish. Bake at 375° for 25 minutes.

HINT: May be served with heated tomato sauce. If using a canned sauce, use a mild flavored one that does not have heavy spices as the spices could overpower the subtle flavor of the nuts.

DESSERTS

Tug Boat Banana Split Cake

When I met Norman in Maui, we were both busy trying to save the whales. It was several months before I found out my mild-mannered friend had once been a cook on a tug boat. He had some interesting recipes to share with me, but this one is sinfully delicious.

Crust

1 package chocolate wafers (crushed)
1 stick margarine, melted

Mix together and press into 9" x 13" pan. Bake at 350° for 8 minutes. Cool.

2nd Layer

2 sticks margarine
2 cups powdered sugar

Beat together for 10 minutes, until very creamy. This must be done for 10 minutes. Spread on cooled crust.

3rd Layer

2–3 bananas

Slice and dip in lemon juice.

Put on top of second layer.

Layer top of bananas with mandarin orange slices (3 small cans, drained).

4th Layer

Large container of whipped topping.

Spread on top of third layer. Top with maraschino cherries.

Chill thoroughly.

Serves 12–15.

Bobbi's No-Fail Chocolate Cake

Being a professional cook and teacher, Bobbi can spend hours over a recipe but she's also a great believer in making it simple whenever she can.

  2 cups sugar
  2 cups flour, sifted
  1 cup water
  1/2 cup buttermilk
  1 tablespoon baking soda
  1/2 teaspoon salt
  2 sticks butter
  5 tablespoons cocoa
  1 teaspoon vanilla
  1 teaspoon cinnamon
  2 eggs, beaten

Shift flour, salt and sugar together. Melt butter, mix with cocoa and water that has been boiled. Pour over dry mixture and blend well. Add buttermilk, eggs and vanilla.

Bake in greased 9" x 13" pan for 15–20 minutes at 350°.

A nice topping for this cake is a cocoa/butter frosting.

Whales are divided into two suborders—those with teeth and those with baleen.

Carrot Cake

2 cups flour
2 cups sugar
2 teaspoons baking powder
2 teaspoons baking soda
1 1/2 teaspoons cinnamon
4 eggs, beaten
1 1/2 cups vegetable oil
1 teaspoon vanilla
3 cups grated carrots
1/2 cup chopped walnuts or pecans

Sift together the first 5 ingredients. Mix eggs, oil and vanilla together. Add to dry ingredients. Mix well. Add carrots and walnuts.

Bake in an ungreased 9" x 13" pan at 350° for 50–55 minutes or until it tests done. Cool. Frost with cream cheese frosting.

Cream Cheese Frosting

4 ounces cream cheese, room temperature
1/2 cup butter or margarine, softened
3 cups powdered sugar
1/2 cup walnuts, chopped

Combine all ingredients. Let cake cool before frosting.

Serves 10–12.

Pound Cake

Be sure to follow directions exactly!

Don't sift anything. Don't grease pan. Don't preheat oven. Don't cream anything. Have all ingredients at room temperature.

Put the following ingredients in a large bowl and beat at high speed for 10 minutes:

2 cups flour
1/2 cup milk
1 1/2 cups sugar
1 tablespoon baking powder
4 eggs
1 tablespoon vanilla
1 cup margarine

Pour into a tube pan and bake at 350° for 1 hour.

This cake is best if it is made one or two days ahead of time. It is quite rich and is wonderful served alone or with a little fresh fruit.

Chocolate/Cherry Cake

1 box chocolate cake mix
1 can cherry pie filling
2 eggs, beaten
1/2 teaspoon almond extract (optional)

Combine all ingredients. Mix well with a large spoon, making sure there are no lumps of dry cake mix. DO NOT use an electric mixer.

Pour into a greased 9" x 13" pan. Bake at 350° for 30–35 minutes or until cake tests done. Cool and serve with whipped topping.

Serves 12.

German Apple Cake

1 box German apple cake mix
2 cups apple pie filling
3 eggs

Combine all ingredients. Mix by hand until very well blended.

Pour into a greased 9" x 13" pan. Bake at 350° for 35–40 minutes or until cake tests done.

Serves 12.

Real Butter Cake

> 3 cups flour
> 1 teaspoon baking powder
> 1 teaspoon salt
> 1/2 teaspoon baking soda

Sift above ingredients together.

> 1 cup butter, unsalted (not margarine)
> 2 cups sugar

Cream together until fluffy and pale yellow

> 4 eggs, blend in one at a time
> 1 cup sour milk (add 2 tablespoons white vinegar to 1 cup milk)

OR

> 1 cup buttermilk
> 2 teaspoons vanilla

Combine and add alternately with the dry ingredients to creamed mixture. Blend well and pour into a greased 10" tube pan or two 9" x 5" x 3" pans. Bake at 325° for 60–65 minutes or until the cake springs back when touched. Run spatula along the edge and stem of the pan. Prick cake with a fork or long skewer. Pour hot sauce over the cake. **Cool before removing from pan.**

Hot Sauce For Butter Cake

> 1 cup sugar
> 1/4 cup water
> 1/2 cup butter (again, must be butter not margarine)

Heat until butter melts but do not boil. Add 1 tablespoon vanilla.

Serves 10.

Is It Fudge Or Is It Brownies?

2 tablespoons cocoa
3/4 cup brown sugar
1/2 cup flour
3/4 cup margarine, melted
1 cup walnuts or pecans, chopped
1 egg, beaten

Mix cocoa and brown sugar together. Add egg, vanilla and margarine, beat until smooth. Add flour and mix well.

Pour into a greased 8" x 8" pan. Bake at 325° for 25 minutes. Cool before cutting.

Makes 9–12 brownies.

These brownies are so rich they are really closer to being fudge, so no need for frosting.

Sheila's "To Die For" Brownies

Like the previous recipe, these brownies are close to fudge but with a slightly different consistency. If you know anyone who wants to do "Death by Chocolate" this is the way to go.

1/4 pound butter or margarine
2 squares unsweetened chocolate
2 eggs slightly beaten
1 cup sugar
1/2 cup flour

Melt chocolate and margarine in a saucepan, over low heat, stirring constantly. Cool slightly and stir in eggs. Add sugar and flour. Stir until well mixed.

Bake in a greased 8" x 8" pan at 350° for 20 minutes.

Makes 9–12 brownies.

Must be made a day ahead and left in the pan in order to cut them.

Nanaimo Bars—White Elk's Version

Nanaimo, Washington may have given birth to this dieter's downfall but there must be as many different recipes for it as there are fish in the river.

Ted White Elk is a sometimes fishing guide in the Pacific Northwest. He uses these bars for energy and as a pacifier when taking tourists out to teach them how to fish for salmon.

1/2 cup butter
3 tablespoons cocoa
1/4 cup white sugar

Melt in a double boiler, stir well, remove from heat. Then add:

1 egg
1/2 cup nuts
1 teaspoon vanilla
1 cup grated coconut
2 cups graham cracker crumbs

Press mixture into a greased 9" x 13" pan and cool in refrigerator. While this is cooling. Cream together:

1/4 cup soft butter
2 tablespoons custard powder (The best one is Birds if you can find this English import)
2 cups icing sugar

Spread evenly over chilled crust, then cool until set.

Melt:

2 ounces unsweetened chocolate
1 tablespoon butter

Drizzle on above mixture, spread evenly and chill. Slice to bite size with a hot knife.

Makes 15–18 bars.

HINT: When trying to bake on a boat you can never get nice even layers unless you wait and do your baking while at anchor. Even then, if the boat rocks slightly, your layers will be uneven due to the motion.

Bread Pudding

2/3 cup brown sugar
4 tablespoons margarine
2 2/3 cups milk
1/2 cup sugar
5 slices buttered bread—cut into 1/2" cubes
4 eggs, beaten
1/2 teaspoon cinnamon

Put brown sugar into the top of a double boiler, spread out to cover the bottom of the pan. Add the margarine which has been cut into pieces so that you can dot it on top of the sugar. Add the bread. Combine the remaining ingredients, mix well and pour over bread. DO NOT MIX. Cover the double boiler and cook over simmering water for 1 hour. (Replace water in pan if it starts to steam away.)

It is done when a sharp knife inserted into the center comes out clean. Allow pudding to cool for a few minutes and then turn onto a platter.

Serves 4.

If you don't have a double boiler you may use a regular sauce pan. Just use a small one for the pudding and place it in a larger pan.

HINT: Diluted non-dairy creamers work well in place of milk. Also, powdered creamers added to skim milk can give you a richer flavor without the fat content. Read the powdered creamer labels carefully as some items have ingredients that are no better than the original item.

Potato Chip Cookies

1 cup butter
1 egg yolk
3/4 cup sugar
1/2 cup crushed potato chips
1 1/2 cups sifted flour
1/2 cup chopped nuts (optional)

Cream butter and sugar, add egg yolk and blend well. Add flour and nuts.

Drop by teaspoonful (1/2 teaspoon) on a greased cookie sheet. Bake at 375° for 12 minutes.

Makes 3–4 dozen.

HINT: To make a soft chocolate chip cookie, add applesauce to the batter.

Baklava

I spent six years as an operating room technician at Methodist Hospital in Omaha. When we weren't operating, we always seemed to be eating.

I made baklava for the first Christmas party I attended, and after that I was assigned to make baklava "in perpetuity."

Through the years I've used several different recipes. Liz Kreekos does not share her favorite baklava recipe very often so I am doubly pleased to be able to include it.

Cold Syrup

Since the syrup has to be cold when it's poured over the baklava, I think it's smart to make it first and allow plenty of time for it to cool. It can be made the day before.

- **6 cups sugar**
- **5 cups water**
- **1/2 cup honey**
- **Juice of 1 lemon**
- **1 stick of cinnamon**
- **3 cloves**
- **Strip of lemon rind**

Mix all ingredients in a sauce pan and stir well. Bring to a boil and cook for 8 to 10 minutes until it's the consistency of pancake syrup. If you use a candy thermometer it should read 210°. Remove from flame, then add 1 jigger whiskey (optional).

Baklava

- **2 pounds finely chopped walnuts. Do not use blender or meat grinder to chop.**
- **1 cup sugar**
- **2 tablespoons cinnamon**
- **1/2 teaspoon nutmeg**
- **2 1/2 pounds melted salt-free butter**
- **2 pounds filo pastry (room temperature)**

Mix walnuts, sugar, cinnamon and nutmeg thoroughly. Set aside.

Melt butter, keep warm. With a pastry brush, butter bottom and sides of an aluminum or stainless steel baking pan 17 1/2" x 11 1/2" x 2 1/2".

Place one filo sheet in the bottom of the pan.

Brush with butter. Sprinkle generously with nut mixture.

Top with another sheet, brush with butter and sprinkle nut mixture over it. Continue alternating filo and nut mix until you have used up nut mixture. You will have eight sheets of filo. Before baking, with a sharp knife, cut baklava in eight long strips. Then cut the strips into diagonal pieces. You can cut 8 to 10 pieces per strip, depending on the size you wish to serve.

Bake in a pre-heated 350° oven for 30 minutes. Reduce heat to 300° and bake for 60 more minutes.

If pastry seems to be browning too soon, cover **loosely** with a piece of foil. Remove from oven and with a ladle, slowly pour **cold** syrup over the hot baklava.

Leave in pan to cool overnight.

Makes 64.

German Chocolate Pie

**4 ounces German chocolate (may substitute dark
  or milk chocolate)**
1/3 cup milk
3 ounces cream cheese, softened
10 ounces whipped topping, thawed
1 Graham Cracker crust

Heat chocolate and 2 tablespoons milk in saucepan over a low heat, stirring constantly until chocolate is melted.

Beat cream cheese and sugar until well mixed. Add remaining milk and chocolate mixture, beat until smooth. Fold in the whipped topping and blend well. Pour into crust.

Freeze for at least 4 hours, until firm. Remove about 30 minutes before serving and refrigerate. Store leftovers in freezer.

Very rich, should serve 10 easily.

Easy as Falling off a Log Pumpkin Pie

I suggest trying this without the sugar as I've found most people don't notice the difference.

29 ounce can pumpkin
2 large eggs
12 ounce can evaporated milk, lowfat is preferable
1/2 cup Bisquick
2 tablespoons margarine
2 1/2 teaspoons pumpkin pie spice
  OR 3/4 teaspoon each cinnamon, allspice and nutmeg
2 teaspoons vanilla
1/2 cup sugar (optional)

Combine all ingredients and beat until smooth and creamy.

Pour into a greased 9" pie pan. Bake in a preheated 350° oven for 55 minutes. Cool. Serve topped with whipped topping.

Serves 8.

Yogurt Pie

This is another easy-to-make recipe that draws many compliments.

1 prepared graham cracker crust
16 ounces lowfat or nonfat fruit yogurt, any flavor
6 ounces frozen whipped topping, thawed

Combine yogurt and whipped topping. Blend until well mixed.

Pour into pie crust and freeze for at least 3 hours. Remove 20 minutes before serving. Freeze any leftovers.

Serves 6–8.

Salmonberry Cream Pie

The salmonberry is a yellow or salmon pink colored berry that grows in Alaska. The first time I saw the bush was on a deserted little island in the middle of Fredrick Sound. The DELPHINUIS had tied up for the night in a snug little cove. The bush can grow to a height of 8 to 10 feet and has small white flowers in the spring. The berries themselves have a flavor slightly similar to a tart raspberry.

6 cups salmonberries (can substitute huckleberries)
2/3 cup sugar
3 tablespoons cornstarch
Water

Force 2 cups of the berries through a sieve.

Add enough water to make 1 1/2 cups mixture. Add sugar and cornstarch. Cook 5 minutes or until thick, stirring constantly. Cool. Place remaining 4 cups of berries into a baked pie shell. If berries are very tart, you can add more sugar to taste. Add the cooled mixture and chill.

Serves 8.

Alaska Berry Pie

Cranberries are used for desserts in the 49th state. You can use fresh, cooked cranberries in place of the salmonberry in the above recipe.

Crunchy Apple Crisp

5 Granny Smith or Pippin apples, peeled,
  cored, thinly sliced
1 1/2 tablespoons lemon juice
1 cup all-purpose flour
3/4–1 cup sugar
1 1/2 teaspoons cinnamon
1/2 cup unsalted butter or margarine, cold, cut into small pieces

Place a layer of apple slices in a greased 8" pan. Sprinkle with a little lemon juice. Repeat the layers until all the apples are in the pan. Combine the flour, sugar and cinnamon in a food processor or a mixing bowl and stir until mixed together. Add the margarine and either process with a steel blade, or use an electric mixer to blend, until the mixture resembles a coarse meal. Press the crumb mixture evenly over the apples. Bake at 350° until the top is golden brown and the apples are tender. About 1 hour. Serve warm.

Serves 6

Super Easy Apple Crisp

4 Granny Smith or Pippin apples, peeled,
  cored and thinly sliced
1 package white or cinnamon apple cake mix
2 sticks margarine—1 stick melted
1 cup brown sugar
cinnamon

Grease a 9" x 13" pan. Arrange apples on the bottom of the pan. Sprinkle with 1/2 cup brown sugar and dot with half of the margarine. Crumble the dry cake mix over the apples. Sprinkle lightly with remaining brown sugar and enough cinnamon to cover apples. Pour about 2/3–1 cup water over the apple mixture, (enough water so that the cake mix is just moistened). Drizzle with 1/4 cup melted margarine. Sprinkle with cinnamon. Bake at 350° for 20-25 minutes or until top is golden brown.

Serves 8–10.

Fresh Peach Surprise

The sweetest peaches I've ever eaten came in a fruit basket in our stateroom on the riverboat DELTA QUEEN. Cruising down the river with the world gliding by your deck chair, is one of the last truly relaxing treats, vacationwise. I've gone around the world by ship and have worked on a cruise ship. As much as I enjoyed both experiences, they did not have the charm of a riverboat.

When we commented on how delicious the DELTA QUEEN's peaches were, and wondered aloud why we never could get the same ones up north, we were told that they "never get that far" as everyone in Georgia gobbles them up!

4 large, ripe peaches

Slice off tops, discard pit. Scoop out enough pulp to leave a nice size hole for filling. Turn upside down to drain while you prepare filling.

Filling

Put peach pulp in a bowl, then add the following:

4 macaroon or almond flavored cookies, crumbled.

Add to this base:

1 cup of vanilla ice cream, softened just enough to mix with fruit and cookies
OR sweetened whipped cream or nondairy whipped topping

Divide between four peaches, fill and replace tops. A spring of mint makes a pretty "stem."

Serves 4.

Bobbi Saper's Chocolate Mousse

1/2 package semi-sweet chocolate pieces
3 eggs, separated
1 teaspoon vanilla

Melt the chocolate over water, remove. With a wooden spoon beat in eggs yolks, and then vanilla.

Beat egg whites until stiff, but not dry, then fold into other ingredients. Spoon into serving dishes, chill for several hours.

This is a rich dessert, but if you want to dress it up, use swirls of whipped cream, dust with shaved chocolate or chocolate sprinkles.

Serves 2

Light Tropical Mousse

Low-fat yogurt easily replaces the higher fat content dairy products in this airy recipe. You can use regular yogurt if you don't care about calories.

8 ounces mandarin orange yogurt
8 ounces banana yogurt
8 ounces pineapple yogurt
2 envelopes unflavored gelatin
1/2 cup unsweetened pineapple juice
3 egg whites
1/3 cup sugar

Have yogurt at room temperature.

Soften gelatin in pineapple juice; cook over low heat, stirring constantly, until gelatin dissolves. Cool.

Mix yogurts thoroughly, blend with gelatin. Refrigerate for about 20 minutes, until mixture has thickened slightly.

Beat egg whites until foamy. Gradually beat in sugar until stiff peaks are formed. Gently fold egg whites into the chilled yogurt mixture.

Refrigerate at least 3–4 hours.

Serves 6.

Jaki's Coffee Soufflé

Jaki grew up in India. I do not know if her food always tasted just a little better because of the spicy anecdotes about her days in India, but I do know this is one dish everyone loves.

A word of caution—I have tried to prepare this on a boat and I have had trouble. Whether it was the humidity, or the gelatin was shelf-old when I purchased it, the soufflé failed.

Dissolve these two ingredients in 1/2 cup HOT water.

1 tablespoon gelatin
1 tablespoon instant coffee

1/2 teaspoon cinnamon (optional)
1 large can evaporated milk (chilled)
1/2 cup sugar
1 teaspoon vanilla

NOTE: When whipping milk or cream, chill beaters and bowl for best results.

Whip milk until stiff peaks form.

Add gelatin-coffee mixture to whipped milk, sugar and vanilla. Stir well and pour into large serving dish or individual dishes.

Decorate top with whipped cream and chopped Heath Bar.

This dessert can be made a day ahead.

Serves 8–10.

Suzanne's Easy Fruit Tart

My good friend Suzanne is a busy registered nurse. Working long hours, she does not have lots of free time to spend making elegant desserts. This fruit tart is a real work of art but is easy to make in a short amount of time. Don't be surprised if people accuse you of sneaking out to the local pastry shop to buy this beautiful creation!

1 roll of refrigerated sugar cookie dough
8 ounces cream cheese, softened
4 1/2 ounces frozen whipped topping, thawed
Fruit: strawberries, raspberries, bananas, mandarin oranges, kiwi fruit (or use your imagination)
1/3 cup sugar
1 tablespoon cornstarch, dissolved in 1/4 cup cold water
1/2 cup orange juice
1 tablespoon lemon juice

Press cookie dough into a greased 12" round pizza pan (you may buy disposable foil pans in any grocery store).

Bake at 350° for about 8 minutes or until just golden brown. Be careful not to overbake. Cool.

Combine cream cheese and whipped topping. Beat until smooth. Spread on top of cooled cookie base. Layer with fruit, in any order you wish.

Glaze

Combine the last 4 ingredients in a small saucepan and boil over a medium-high heat for 1 minute, stirring constantly.

Cool for about 5 minutes then spoon over the fruit.

NOTE: It is very important that this topping is cooked thoroughly. If you under-cook it, you could get a filmy, unappetizing looking sauce. Omit the sauce if you prefer.

Chill until ready to serve.

Serves 10.

Easy-Cheesy Lemon Bars

1 package lemon cake mix
1/2 cup unsalted butter or margarine, melted
1 egg, slightly beaten
1 package lemon frosting mix
   (if you can't find lemon flavored mix use a white frosting mix
   and add about 1/4 cup lemon juice or to taste)
8 ounces cream cheese, softened
2 eggs

Combine cake mix, butter or margarine and 1 egg. Mix with fork until moist. Pat cake mixture into the bottom of a greased 9" x 13" pan.

Blend frosting mix into cream cheese. Reserve 1/2 cup of this mixture.

Add 2 eggs to remaining frosting mixture. Beat 4 minutes at high speed. Spread over cake mix.

Bake at 350° for 30–40 minutes or until light brown. Cool and spread with reserved frosting mix.

These freeze very well. In fact I prefer eating them when they've been frozen and thawed for only 10–15 minutes so they're still slightly frozen.

Makes 12–15 bars.

Hints For Seasoning Without Salt

Seasoning Without Salt

There are many satisfactory substitutes for salt. It's just a question of finding the ones you prefer.

Asparagus: Lemon juice, pepper.

Corn: Green pepper, tomato, pimento, cayenne.

Green beans: onion, marjoram, lemon juice, dill. For an unusual flavor, you might want to try a clove or two.

Peas: mint, dill, nutmeg, onion, red pepper.

Potatoes: dill, onion, mace, green pepper, caraway seeds.

Winter Squash: applesauce, brown sugar, cranberries, cinnamon, nutmeg, ginger.

Zucchini: Dill, onions, basil.

Tomatoes: basil, celery, onion, pepper, dill, oregano.

Beef: basil, bay leaf, marjoram, onion, cumin, mustard, oregano, thyme, nutmeg, paprika.

Chicken: Cranberries, marjoram, paprika, savory, tarragon, thyme.

Lamb: Mint, garlic, rosemary.

Pork: Applesauce, mint, sage, thyme, vinegar.

Veal: Apricots, bay leaf, ginger, lemon juice, marjoram.

Fish: Lemon juice, bay leaf, dill, dry mustard, green onion, paprika.

Eggs: Curry powder, cayenne, dill, mustard, garlic, green onion, peppers-red or green, onion, paprika, parsley.

Noodles: Basil, poppyseed, pepper, caraway seed, rye seed.

Pasta: Onion, garlic, pepper.

About the Author

Sharon Nogg follows the Humpback Whales of the Pacific. A senior naturalist for Earthtrust in Honolulu, Nogg works in Hawaii during the winter months. In the summer, she is a naturalist for Holland American Lines in Southeast Alaska, an area that features Humpback, Minke and Orca whales.

A former field representative for the American Humane Society's Hollywood Office and a zookeeper at the Playboy Mansion West, Nogg also has worked with the Center for Whale Research in Friday Harbor, Washington.

Her culinary skills were honed working for a caterer in Beverly Hills. Following her work at Friday Harbor, Biological Journeys hired her as a full-time cook on their boat the DELPHINUS.

The Audubon Society has selected some of Nogg's wild life photographs for their new guidebook.

Available at your local bookstore OR
ORDER DIRECT Call 1-800-627-9919

☐ YES, I want ____ copy/copies of **Whale Watcher's Cookbook** for $9.95 plus $2.50 shipping.

☐ YES, please send my friend ____ copy/copies of **Whale Watcher's Cookbook** at $9.95 plus $2.50 shipping.

A portion of the royalties will aid conservation groups.

Method of payment

☐ Check for $_____ to:
Media Publishing
2440 'O' Street, Suite 202
Lincoln, Nebraska 68510

☐ Charge my credit card
  ☐ Visa   ☐ MasterCard

Account # _____
Exp. Date _____
Signature _____
Phone # _____

Bill to:_____
_____
_____
_____

Gift/Ship to: _____
_____
_____
_____

Available at your local bookstore OR
ORDER DIRECT Call 1-800-627-9919

☐ YES, I want ____ copy/copies of **Whale Watcher's Cookbook** for $9.95 plus $2.50 shipping.

☐ YES, please send my friend ____ copy/copies of **Whale Watcher's Cookbook** at $9.95 plus $2.50 shipping.

A portion of the royalties will aid conservation groups.

Method of payment

☐ Check for $_____ to:
Media Publishing
2440 'O' Street, Suite 202
Lincoln, Nebraska 68510

☐ Charge my credit card
  ☐ Visa   ☐ MasterCard

Account # _____
Exp. Date _____
Signature _____
Phone # _____

Bill to: _____
_____
_____
_____

Gift/Ship to: _____
_____
_____
_____